Jess,
You are su
bright star. Keep
on shining!
— Love, Cari

Just when
I fell in lae
in Aja. Co
so Miss You
. xoxo
Peace & Lae
Julie Green

Joyous
Freedom
Journal

Jess,
what a blessing
to have you in
my life! I am
so thrilled for you
and your journey!
always remember you
are loved! Albianne♡

Love you Jess!
Call me anytime
562.209.7802
Toni
Wallace

Jess,
Wow, you
brought it all - all
of what you brought made
the difference! I love you
and honor your path
Love
RBB

Jess!
Who loves ya, baby?!
I do! We do! I'm
not saying goodbye
Life I know we'll
going to see you
still. Sending you
love + blessings
Always, dear
friend.
♡ Kim

Joyous

Freedom

Journal

Jess —
FREEDOM, by,
THAT'S you!!
ALWAYS —
Chris
(REMEMBER THIS
on your Journey!!)

JESS,
So excited for you as
you take this Ride
on your magical carpet
Journey.
Love you
NICKI

Petra Weldes

Christian Sørensen

Dearest Jess,
Thank you for ALL you've
given us: Time, Talent + Treasure!
Blessings to your next chapter.

Spiritual Living Press
Golden, Colorado

Enjoy life
and know
you are always
loved and
missed!
Chris

Spiritual Living Press
573 Park Point Drive
Golden, Colorado 80401-7042

Printed in USA
Published October 2009

ISBN 0-972184-9-4
ISBN13 978-0-9727184-9-3

Design by Randall Friesen

For my beloved Susan and my son, Jason,
who make every year joyous and free!
Petra

This journal is dedicated to all the members,
throughout all its years, of The Seaside
Center for Spiritual Living,
who have supported me through
my spiritual explorations.

Kalli, my wife and Trevor, my son,
who put up with me writing through
all our trips this last year
Christian

Forward

Pierre Teilhard de Chardin said, "Joy is the most infallible sign of the presence of God." The soul craves freedom and joy—the freedom of self-expression, the joy of being. This is, actually, our inheritance and our birthright. There are many ways to express joy and experience freedom: living one's purpose, finding one's passion, healing past hurts, living in the moment, making new choices, and building lives centered in Spirit and based on spiritual principles. Yet, there are certainly times when this is not how we live or what we experience.

We believe in personal healing, spiritual transformation, and the revelation of the true, magnificent, and glorious Self. However, during times when we experience something other than these truths, we notice that it takes practice to recapture the joyous freedom of our true self-expression. Often, people work hard to free themselves from their constraints. Yet, when freed of difficulties, joy isn't guaranteed. Sometimes, all we get is relieved from the weight of our burdens. But we all want more than to simply survive. We want our lives to joyously thrive and freely flourish!

We invite you to run free through this world with joy, realizing you freely create your joyous heaven on earth. Your joy and your freedom not only bless you, but also bless everyone around you. As your life becomes one of Joyous Freedom, you respond to and interact with the people in your life in a whole new way. This changes everything, including the emerging reality of humanity itself. Each of us is a point of inspiration and light on Indra's Net, the web of life in which we are all inextricably bound. When one light brightens, lifts free of its fear and self-imposed limitation, and shouts with joy, it can not help put spread that light around, lifting the entire web!

May you be free and joyous all year!

Petra Weldes and Christian Sørensen

How to Use This Book

Joyous Freedom Journal was written directly to you with the intention to help you engage, practice, respond, and explore, daily, new ideas that will free you from those things in your life that keep you stuck.

As an individual

As you read each thought for the day, journal, doodle, draw, or comment in whatever way allows you to explore the idea presented. Where are you with it? What do you think about it? How can you engage with it? And most importantly, how can you practice freeing yourself to experience the joyous life that is the Divine Intention wanting to manifest in, through, and as *you*?

As a book club or small group

Each month has a theme that is broken into daily topics. Groups may meet weekly or monthly to explore the topics and themes. Mediate on the theme together. Share what you discover in your journal. Discuss deeper practices that will help you and the members of your group. Pray for each other during the meetings, and as prayer partners, between meetings.

As a Spiritual Community

Using a journal like this allows your whole community to be on the same page for the whole year. Joyous Freedom can be a wonderful annual theme to focus your year around. The theme for the month can also be utilized by the children and youth. Each week's lesson can be based on the topic within each month's theme. When there are five weeks in a month, this allows for an additional deepening into the overall idea being explored. The individual days provide excellent material, quotes, and ideas for weekly lessons or presentations.

Weekly or monthly study groups can be formed, as mentioned above, in support of engaging with the material and practicing it more deeply. These can take place at your community location, or in members' homes for a more intimate, community-building experience.

Free to
Catch the Vision

January 1-8
Joyous New Beginnings

January 9-17
The Joy of Knowing What You Want

January 18-24
The Joy of Knowing Who You Are

January 25-31
The Joy of Living Your Dreams

Janus—Your Choice

Imagine being able to see into the future with the wisdom of the past. The first day of the year invites you to do just that. The Roman mythical character, Janus, is associated with beginnings and endings, gates, doorways, and transitions. Associated with transition, he is depicted with two faces looking out in opposite directions. Janus was honored at planting and harvest times, weddings, and births. Also honored at the first hour of each day and the first day of the month, he has a month named after him—January.

Today, you can cross the threshold of what has been and enter a new phase of your life. Today can be no different than any other day, or you can choose today to align with the collective planetary energy of all those who are choosing today as the beginning of a greater yet-to-be. You stand with the wisdom of all your previous years, looking out upon the infinite possibilities that lie before you. You face the choice between two types of years, both with unlimited potential. Are you going to perpetuate what has been or claim something more? Life is neutral. It won't choose for you. Life only supports your choices; you are free to bring the color and joy you want into your world.

Go ahead—be bold, and write out your intentions for this new year of yours!

JOURNAL:

Starting Fresh

Every day offers a new opportunity to start fresh. When you wake up each morning, you have a brand new set of twenty-four hours. No matter what happened yesterday, it's over. Today, you can start anew with your choices and commitments, becoming the person you really want to be.

Every year also offers a new opportunity to start fresh. In January, you have a brand new set of twelve months, fifty-two weeks, 365 days to fill with new opportunities, new possibilities, new commitments, and new ways of seeing, being, and doing. What an exciting adventure each new day and each new year presents to you!

Journal about your fresh start this year, thinking about who you want to be and what you want to do differently.

JOURNAL:

Opening to Possibility

New beginnings are wonderful! An entire world opens to you. New possibilities and changes you have wanted to make are right here on the horizon. Now is the time to remember that you are free to choose whatever you want your life to be. You're not stuck with choices you've made in the past. You can recommit to them, or you can choose something new.

One of the most comforting things to remember about Spirit is that It is *infinite*. This means there is an infinite number of possibilities available to you when you allow yourself to explore them without worry, fear, or trying to figure it all out.

Starting a new year is an invitation to look at where you want to be in life. Take some time to dream about this, and then write down what you'd like your life to be like.

JOURNAL:

Making Powerful Choices

You are free to choose anything you want to choose. You are free to change anything you want to change. But the most powerful choices are those that are in alignment with your spiritual truth—with who you are. They are the ones that actively promote growth, love, joy, and wholeness for yourself and for those around you.

When you look at life with a fresh eye, you may see that your previous choices no longer support you, nor are they good for those you love and care about. Now is the time to make a powerful new choice.

Take some time today to journal about the choices you want to make. Identify those that are most aligned with love, joy, growth, and wholeness.

JOURNAL:

Endless Opportunities

Occasionally, you feel like you are facing an either/or choice. At those times, you may fear making the wrong choice or feel you've missed an opportunity by not choosing something different. Since God is infinite, the good news is that there are endless choices. There aren't only two choices—"either" and "or." In God, there are at least three, four, even five more alternatives! There can't be just one opportunity that you've now missed; in God, there are endless opportunities. Another will come along as you keep yourself focused and watch out for it.

Often, the only thing keeping you from seeing other alternatives or opportunities is your unwillingness to think outside the box or your lack of imagining other possible solutions.

What other alternatives might you have right now? Journal today about the opportunities and possibilities, letting yourself be free and even silly. Notice what emerges.

JOURNAL:

Are You Ready?

Where are you going if you have no purpose? It is written: "Without vision, the people perish." When you become aware of your true identity, you move into right relationship with the world. Consciousness is the creative avenue through which the power flows. According to spiritual principle, it is done unto you as you believe. The law is neutral and responds with an amazing, infinite ability to manifest according to the direction given it.

When you are in tune with the Infinite, the instruction you give comes from a higher vision than your earthly mind. Step away from your worldly needs, and open up to your soul's desire. Find the courage to trust the vision, and you will find all your worldly needs taken care of, even before you know what they are.

The Intelligence that guides the Universe is ready to give guidance to your life. Are you ready?

JOURNAL:

Seeing the World Anew

Spiritual principles teach that much of your experience of life is based on your viewpoint of how you see the world. There is great wisdom in asking yourself, "Do I see the cup as half full or half empty?" Before you can decide what you really want, you must take a clear look at what you already have and how your life is already working.

It may be that the things you want to change, fix, or are unhappy with are actually fine. It may simply be the way you are looking at them. Do you think you're too fat or old, in a bad relationship, or unappreciated at work? The first thing to do is question if that's really true.

Take some quiet time today to really look at the things you want to change. Write down some ways you might be able to look at them differently.

JOURNAL:

Opening your Heart to Joy

Open-heartedness is necessary for joy to flow. Yet being open-hearted can seem like a vulnerable and naïve place from which to live.

Joy is a feeling of aliveness and expansion. Joy bubbles out when you are personally fulfilled or when you celebrate fulfillment in someone else's life. It is almost impossible to experience or express joy if you are anxious, envious, protective, or feeling constricted or dead. Resentment, judgment, lack of forgiveness, hurt, pettiness, gossip, and comparison are other states that obstruct you from your joy.

Turning yourself around with positive, expansive thoughts and feelings will open your heart and release more of your joy. Journal about where you can be more open-hearted.

JOURNAL:

What do you want?

"What do you want?" can be a challenging question. You are taught not to want for yourself, but to give to others; to be happy with what you have; not to be greedy; not to think you deserve anything more than you already have. Then, you are told what to want by your parents, teachers, friends, advertisements, and the world around you! Additionally, there are the habits you've gotten into—desiring a snack, a cigarette, or a drink. Underneath all of that is what you *truly* want.

What is true to your nature? How do you desire to express life? In which way do you give your gift to the world? Learning to ask yourself the question "What do I really want right now?" begins to access your inner knowing about what's healthy for you, what's in alignment with who you are, and how you can meaningfully contribute.

JOURNAL:

Having It All

You are free to do, be, and have whatever you choose. However, trying to have it all can become overwhelming and exhausting, especially when you try to have it all at once. "Having it all" means you can have anything on which you choose to put your mental energy and attention. But it doesn't mean you can have everything you want all at the same time.

Today, journal about all the things you want. First, decide if these are things you sincerely want or if they are things you think you *should* want. Then, begin making choices about which ones you are willing to commit to now and which ones you can imagine yourself experiencing at another time in your life.

JOURNAL:

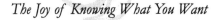

The Green Flash

In the late afternoon of a crystal clear day, just as the last of the sun dips into the ocean, you just might see a green flash. This illusive, rare phenomenon is not that illusive if you know what you are looking for. There have been times, sitting on my porch with friends watching the sunset, when this green flash-of-a-moment occurs. When I ask my friends if they just saw that flash on the horizon, they look at me as if I'm crazy, thinking it's a joke. What I've come to realize is that unless my friends know what they are looking for, they can be looking right at it and not see it.

This kind of "not seeing" is true when we don't have eyes to see heaven on earth. The degree of our demonstration is the degree of awareness that we bring to any situation. Our world becomes heaven when we allow God to fulfill Itself as our expression.

Where in your life would you like to see more Divine Expression?

JOURNAL:

I Spy

When traveling, my young son, Trevor, sometimes gets bored. When this happens, my wife, Kalli, pulls out a magazine with lots of pictures. She'll choose an obscure object on the page for my son to spot and say, "I spy." Other times, when waiting for a plane at the airport, she'll choose an object in the terminal. It's amazing how he can peruse the scene or the environment and come into alignment with what Mom has spotted. No matter how abstract the object may be, Trevor somehow tunes in and is able to find it.

Imagine if we, with the same amount of determination, focus on what our heavenly Mother/Father sees? Our capacity to see in this way depends on *our* willingness, not Spirit's. Life presents us with all options at all times; it's a matter of the position from which we look. That looking can come from knowing that God already knows the answer. It's just a matter of seeing as God sees.

What good things is life seeing for you?

JOURNAL:

Over the Edge

I remember the first time I repelled down the side of a waterfall. Leaning backwards over the edge of the 165-foot face seemed totally contrary to all my natural instincts of self-preservation. Yet, there was a part of me that had a faith greater than all my logical concerns. I knew the ropes would hold me, and the people with me had successfully accomplished this many times before. Could I get out of my head as to how to do this, actually move beyond the theory and prove it works? Did I have the faith to leap off the cliff and trust the support?

We study spiritual principles and learn theories about how to create wonders in our life when confronted with challenges, but do we have the faith to step off the edge of what we know and trust the spiritual support system? The only way to know for sure is to take that leap of faith and move from theory to practice. The only way you'll know the joy and exhilaration of taking conscious control of your subconscious constraints is to go beyond the edge of where you've been before.

JOURNAL:

Cooking Up Life

When cooking, you add a dash of this and a dash of that, and, *viola*, you have a delectable delight. If your partner wants to put a dash of his or her spice into the pot, but you don't want that flavor, things can really heat up in the kitchen! It's not that his or her contribution is wrong—it's just different.

Part of the epicurean wonder is how diverse flavors can maintain their integrity without losing their identity, while at the same time contributing to a unique dish. When creating your day or your life, you may find a lot of well-meaning contributors in the kitchen of your world who would like to contribute to what you're cooking. You know what you like best, and what goes into the mixture is your distinctive choice. Each selection you make brings a distinguishing value.

What do you want to add to your creation, and what contribution is someone attempting to make on your behalf that you don't want?

JOURNAL:

You Have Authority

It's funny how often people start advice with, "They say..." It's alarming how often we wonder, "What will they think?" Who is this "they," and who invited them to the party of your life anyway? It's *your* life, and you're the one who has to live it, not anyone else. No one else cares as much about your life as you do. And no one can give to life what you have to give.

You have authority over the choices in your life. You are capable of learning whatever you need to know to make you own choices. You are able to set whatever intentions you choose, as long as they harm no one else.

Journal about to whom you give your authority away.

JOURNAL:

Giving Power Away

No one can know you as well as you know yourself. Don't give your power away to some outside authority, even if it is a medical or spiritual practitioner. It's alright to get a different perspective or a professional point of view. But remember, it's *theirs* and not the deep knowing that comes from being connected to your body and soul. If you find yourself being belittled, made to feel wrong, punished or ostracized for how you feel, then it might be time to move beyond that relationship.

When you find yourself holding on to a "master" for direction or advice, it's time to start asking yourself if the master has become your source of guidance, or if he or she is pointing you to yourself to hear your true, inner guidance system. No one has the blueprint for your life of joy. It is only by keeping your independence, freedom, and personality that you will ever be fully expressed.

How in the past—or now—have you given your power away to another individual?

JOURNAL:

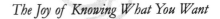

Quick 3

When you are out of sorts, not sleeping at night, or unable to get focused in life, try the quick three: 1) check your diet; 2) rein in your mind; 3) make your environment safe. It's inevitable that there will be disturbances in life from time to time. Do what you can to make your home a sanctuary, so you can get away from environmental upheavals like financial crises, climate disasters, workplace annoyances, and other outside challenges. Build yourself an altar at home, so you have a constant reminder of a higher power.

Food that is lacking life, devoid of nutritional value, cannot be expected to replenish vital, life-enhancing nurturance. Make sure your body is getting sufficient exercise, so it can eliminate toxic energy that otherwise will be processed in the early morning. When your body and environment are working, it's a lot easier to notice where your mind has decided to run on its own. Take a third-person perspective to see where your thinking is running rampant or where it's plotting, victimizing, agonizing, or stressing out. Cut off the parasitical devouring of your life force. Go back to meditating, connecting, and remembering who is in charge of you world. (A clue: it's not your body!)

How can you arrange your world so you can come back into balance?

JOURNAL:

Dissolving Delusions

Delusions can be dissipated in a moment. A state of mind is transitory. As Solomon was told, "This too shall pass." By forgetting who you truly are, you can fall into separateness and get lost in the smallness of worries. It's as if you had been kidnapped and were being forced to go where you don't want to go. Yet, once the kidnappers are gone, you are free to go where you want. When the kidnapping delusions of the mind are gone, you are free to see the infinite possibilities.

There is a freedom beyond perception, if you are willing to go there. This kind of clarity will awaken a compassion beyond judgment. To dissolve delusions, you must choose to rid your mind of any of the perpetual beliefs in limitation, and remember your true Divine nature.

JOURNAL:

Believe in Yourself

Spirit is Infinite. Therefore, there are infinite ways in which Spirit incarnates. One of those ways is *you*. You are a unique and precious incarnation of Spirit, and you are necessary to the Universe. If you weren't here, Spirit would be incarnated as "infinity minus one." And that's not possible.

Believe in yourself as a precious incarnation. "God don't make no junk," the saying goes. The unique set of talents, tendencies, experiences, and ideas that make you who you are, is perfect. Therefore, you are every good thing you desire.

How do you believe in yourself? Write about the love and support you are willing to give yourself.

JOURNAL:

Steps of Duality

What is the nature of the Divine that constantly seeks to pour Itself through you? The shift from mental belief to spiritual understanding is the revelation of God in you. There is no discord in Spirit. Discord has no avenue for its manifestation other than the misaligned thought pattern of the moment. Error has no memory and no way to perpetuate itself through the human scene other than through duality. Healing takes place when we come to realize our true relationship with the One. In this understanding, there can be no otherness; all distortions are neutralized and return to the nothingness from whence they came.

There cannot be any element of dis-ease in the Mind of God. Relax the conscious mind's struggle to get it right, and allow the flow of Good that is already having its way with you. Rest in the awareness that it is Spirit's good pleasure to give you the kingdom. Every time you become more consciously aware of the Presence, some aspect of the personal self dissolves, and Universal Mind finds a clear path to be expressed.

Is there any area of your life in which you could use a clearer expression of God?

JOURNAL:

Error of the Ages

Joel Goldsmith wrote, "The error of the ages is the idea of seeking God, contacting God, communing with God, praying to God." It's easy to fall back into the old, collective belief that Spirit is something to reach out to, rather than a Divine Intelligence dwelling within. When one awakens to the realization that Spirit is not out there somewhere to be found, but within to be realized, healing happens, not because of one's direction, but because there cannot be anything unlike God.

Spend time contemplating and meditating on the concept of Omnipresence, and truly embody what *everywhere* really means. Wherever you bring your awareness, the fullness of God is already there. You can make it difficult and continue seeking, or you can make it easy and realize you are part of the Infinite. With this realization comes all the blessings of ease and grace.

JOURNAL:

Spirit is the One Source

There is a vast, infinite pool of Presence and Peace at the center of the Universe. It is the Infinite Reality from which all creation springs. It is the source of Life itself, and it is the impulsion of Life to express, grow, and become through all creation. This impulse is the Love of God—Spirit pouring Itself into and throughout all creation.

This same life, at the center of all life, is your life right now. The very life which is the love of God pouring Itself into form is forever pouring Itself in, through, and as you.

Spend time in silence reflecting on these truths. How does it feel to know that your very life is sourced in the Infinite Life of God?

JOURNAL:

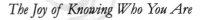

Perfection or Progress

As you let go of the need for perfection and remain content with your progress, life becomes more fun and joy-filled. You are an unfolding state of consciousness in which the outer world reflects the inner. The outer reflects where you must do your spiritual work. When there is discord, it's because you believe there is some power apart from God. When you truly believe God is all there is, the issues dissolve.

If you truly know that in the Divine Presence there is no discord, you will embrace it as valuable information for your progress along the path. Attempting perfection adds unnecessary strain and removes joy. When listening to the joyless voice for direction, you can be assured that it's not leading you to happiness. It doesn't know Joy's way. Honor yourself for your progress, stay open to learn what life has to show you, and you'll give up the need for perfection for the joy in your progress.

When do you remove joy in order to pursue perfection?

JOURNAL:

Let It Be in You

The magnificent works done by the man, Jesus, were a direct result and activity of the mind which was in him and of the One who sent him. It's all too easy to slip into the belief that your mind is separate from that of the Infinite. Not that duality is real; it's our *belief* in duality that creates the issue of otherness. To regain the healing faculties that Jesus exemplified and told us we, too, can exercise, we must surrender the personal concept of "I am doing it" and return to the true "I am it."

With the expanded awareness of universality in the Divine Consciousness, there is no longer an overcoming of the human condition. We are not using a bigger power to overcome a smaller power, because there is only One Power and One Presence in which nothing else can exist that is apart or separate from God. In direct proportion to the degree of perception you embody of your Oneness, you, too, will be able to do the work—and even greater.

JOURNAL:

The Freedom of the Now

Now is the only time you have. This moment is the only time in which you have the freedom to choose who you want to be, how you want to behave, what you want to think, and what you are willing to focus on. In this moment, you are completely free to be, act, react, or think anything you choose.

Imagine exercising this freedom. Think about right now, this very moment. You are free. What are you choosing?

JOURNAL:

Flying Stingrays

Every now and then, some of the wonderful, unseen qualities that lay just below the surface make themselves known to the visible world. I was once sailing with my family and friends, when all around our boat there appeared hundreds of stingrays, flying out of the water and flapping their wings as if they were attempting to fly through the air. They twisted and turned, diving back into the water and putting on an amazing show. This display of nature was engaging, entertaining, and a reminder of how much more there is to life that we don't typically get to see.

When I see new wonders of life, I'm reminded of the Infinite Intelligence of the universe that has created everything without any advice from me. In seeing new and wondrous expressions of Spirit, I remember my only true desire is to experience God and to realize It as my life. It is this realization that becomes the demonstration of Good in my world. In embodying the activity of God, I must let go of what I think things should look like on the surface and open up to the Divine surprises of life that far exceed what I know.

Where in your life are you ready for some Divine surprises?

JOURNAL:

January 27

Yes, You Can

You are a magnificent, radiant being of light and love, because you are made in the image and likeness of Life Itself. This means you are creative, loving, and powerful. You can choose to live a life that is meaningful, fulfilling, and has purpose and joy. You can create a life that grows your spirit while you give your gift to the world. You can be happy with who you are, while continuing to grow and stretch into the more you can become.

Yes, you can!

Begin today by journaling some affirmations about the truth of your life and the gifts you bring to the world. Write positive statements of truth, then re-read them until you believe them.

JOURNAL:

Time to Drop In

There is a bumper sticker in the surfing world that says, "Eddie would go." Eddie Aikau was a waterman, a big wave rider, and the first lifeguard at Waimea Bay on the North Shore of Oahu. He was courageous in his willingness to paddle out and drop into the monstrous moving mountains of water. He knew that letting go of control and going with the enormous, energtic flow of a wave was an indescribable experience.

Are you willing to drop into the indescribable experience of Spirit? Do you hear your companions on this adventure yelling, "This is your wave, your experience. Get moving. It's yours to catch. Let go. Drop in!"? Can you hear them shouting, "Go for it. You can do it!"? This encouragement is a blessing for you, because it says "yes" to this adventurous ride through life. It reflects back to you the possibilities and potentials you would never know unless you unleashed the power of the wave moving through your world. Your crew is here to encourage you, to help you up when you wipe out, and hoot, howl, and celebrate your awesome ride.

Where in your life are you holding back when you know it's time to "drop in?"

JOURNAL:

Life is on Your Side

The Universal Laws of Life are the ways that Spirit creates and incarnates into form. You simply have to observe life to see that these laws are consistently about greater life, greater growth, and greater expression. See how the grass grows in the smallest crack in the sidewalk? See how the rose blooms, even when no one notices it? See how the chick learns to fly and the foal learns to run? The law of growth is inherent in every seed, drawing to it exactly what it needs to sprout, grow, flower, and bear fruit.

The Universal Laws of Life are forever seeking to say "yes" to more life, more growth, and more expression in your life, too. What would you do if you knew that you couldn't fail? Remember that Life is always on your side.

JOURNAL:

Creation of the Heart

Worriers energetically and graphically color their minds with pictures of their challenges in glorious detail. Then, they go into the world and get validation from anyone who agrees with them about how awful things are. It's just as easy to see oneself creating a heart's dream as it is to see losing it. The world has a way of creating space for individuals who seem to know where they are going. Whatever comes your way on this journey through life, remember: it's just what you need. What you attract into your life is part of your soul's personal curriculum. So stop judging things as bad and get on with creations of the heart.

Your vision becomes clear when you look into your heart. Creation doesn't come by vaguely saying everything is good. It comes from tuning in to the power within you that knows how to create and by taking the action that brings it about. It's not a matter of believing in the heart's dream; it's a matter of believing and acting from it as if it's already so.

How would your life be if you faced your challenges from the place that you knew your dreams were already a reality?

JOURNAL:

Allowing Spirit to Move

Imaging possibilities and setting your intention creates the pathway through which the Universal Law can manifest your heart's desires. This is where you step out of the way. Your job is to set the intention and hold the vision, not manage the "how-will-this-happen." That's the job of the Universal Law that governs all creation.

When you allow Spirit to flow through you, your life opens to the "miraculous" coincidences and serendipities that make your dreams come true. This means that you let go of figuring out *how* something will happen, and you trust that it *will* happen. Allowing Spirit to unfold in your life allows you to move with peace and assurance.

Look at the ways you try to manipulate life, and journal about how it would feel to simply allow Spirit to move freely through you.

JOURNAL:

February

Free to Love

God is Love

Every spiritual faith and tradition uses *love* as a synonym for *God*. We have a deep intuition that the impulsion of life itself is love—the love of a mother for her child, the love of a person for his or her mate, the love of the flowers for the sun, the love of the dolphin for the waves. Everywhere we look, we see love in action.

This same intuition teaches us that the Universe Itself runs on love. God's desire to express and become through incarnation is a similarly profound act of love. God has given Itself—all of its qualities and attributes—to become you *as* you. That is how much God loves. And that love pours through you as your love into the world.

How do you experience the Love of God?

JOURNAL:

Loving God

What do you imagine when you think of God? Imagine a Power and a Presence so vast it's incomprehensible, yet so intimate that it's as close as your breath, and so present that it's in all creation. This power and presence is your very life. It is the presence of love in all creation. It is the presence of creativity, joy, harmony, and peace. And, it is a universal power so perfect that it knows how to create and become anything you can imagine.

When you fall in love with God, you recognize these truths and celebrate them with your heart, soul, and mind. Loving God means letting these truths be the path you follow. Loving God means allowing yourself to be awed by the Power and comforted by the Presence.

What does loving God look, feel, or seem like to you? When is it easy for you to love God? When is it not so easy?

JOURNAL:

Loving the World

Seeing the sun peek through the trees, watching the world awaken, it's easy to remember what a magnificent home this planet is to us. Watching a waterfall or the ocean waves. Hearing the wind and smelling the earth. These things remind us that the Earth is our place of refuge, nourishment, and creative expression.

We remember that we are one with everything we see, with all beings everywhere, and with all life. Whatever we do to another, we do to ourselves.

Everyday, you have the choice to love the world or neglect it. You have the choice to take the time to care for your planet, or to simply do what's easy and convenient. Love requires something from you. It requires your care, compassion, and thoughtful action.

What are you doing to love the world? What can you do to love it more?

JOURNAL:

Practicing Loving-kindness

May you be filled with Loving Kindness.
May you be well.
May you be peaceful and at ease.
May you be happy.

This Buddhist prayer is a powerful mantra to use whenever you are faced with a challenging person or see someone in need. Sending them this prayer with the intention of your heart can make a huge difference, even when they are not aware of it.

Practice this prayer in tense situations, in times of anger, sadness, or hurt. Practice this prayer when you see a homeless person, a criminal, or an addict. Practice this prayer by sending it to your four-legged, winged, swimming, and creepy-crawling relations, wherever you see them. Practice this prayer at home, in your office, your community, and for your government.

JOURNAL:

Love is the Answer

Remember the "what-would-Jesus-do" bracelets? Wouldn't it be great if you had one that said, "what-would-Love-do"? What would Love do when you want to tell someone the truth? What would Love do when someone needed help or support? What would Love do when you're feeling overwhelmed? What would Love do when you want to celebrate your joy? What would Love do when you feel you're not growing? What would Love do when you want to create a new business? What would Love do when you want to express your creativity? What would Love do when you want to give the gift of yourself to the world?

Anytime you are confronted with a situation you aren't sure how to handle, ask yourself this question and see what answer emerges. Take some time to explore this thought in your journal.

JOURNAL:

Making Room for Love

Love grows slowly and matures over time. Love requires nurturing and space in which to flourish. Love takes attention and can't be fit into convenient moments. Do you have room for love in your life?

Make room for love by creating spaciousness in your calendar. Set aside time for your loved ones. Make room for love by creating spaciousness in your mind. Set aside complaints, gripes, and criticism. Make room for love by creating space in your heart. Set aside unforgiveness, grudges, and hurts.

Making room for love makes room for Spirit to permeate your relationships, bringing vitality, richness, and joy. Journal about how you can make more room for love in your life.

JOURNAL:

Allowing Love In

When you dance with a partner, one person leads and the other follows. Being the follower means you allow the other person to take you where they want, trusting them to keep you safe and make you look beautiful. Allowing Love into your life means you follow where Love leads, letting it take you where it wants, trusting that you will be safe and feel beautiful.

If you are used to being the leader, following can be a challenge. If you are used to being in control, allowing Love to lead can be challenging, too. Yet Love comes from the very Heart of God. It is the primary impulsion of the Universe, of Life itself. Allowing Love in allows you to live in the very heart of God. It allows Spirit to lead you through the dance of Life.

JOURNAL:

When the Going Gets Tough

Love is a decision, a commitment you make everyday. It's easy when you're happy with someone or experience that "in love" feeling. But what about when you don't feel love towards someone?

First, remember that both of you are children of God, incarnations of Love and Life Itself. Second, remember what you love about the other person. Third, commit to being a benevolent presence in that person's life, regardless of what they are doing. Then, you let them have the space they need to work through whatever is going on for them. (But this does not mean you become a doormat or accept abuse.)

Journal about your decision to love and your commitment to love others, yourself, the world, and God.

JOURNAL:

Let Yourself to Be Loved

Are you suspicious when someone is nice to you, wondering what they want? Are you so busy giving to others that you don't let others give to you? Are you uncomfortable taking compliments or receiving praise? Do you dismiss offers of help or gifts?

In nature, all things circulate—water, air, life itself. Circulation is necessary to prevent stagnation and rot. As important as it is to love others, it is equally important to allow others to love you. Love your neighbor *as* yourself—not more than, not instead of, but as much as! This allows for a free flowing exchange of love.

Allowing yourself to be loved allows Spirit to refill your cup so you have more to give. It also reminds you that, as a child of God, you are worthy to receive the very gifts of heaven itself. There is nothing you need to do to earn love; simply being yourself is enough.

JOURNAL:

Mirror, Mirror on the Wall

There's an old saying: "When you point a finger at someone else, three fingers are pointing back at you." This is one of the greatest challenges—and gifts—that a relationship can offer. While there certainly are exceptions, like abuse or neglect, usually when you accuse someone of being defensive or cold, uncaring or clingy, you are actually projecting onto them the very thing you are doing yourself.

It takes a fair amount of courage and willingness to be truthful with yourself. Are you unwilling to feel your own negative feelings and are, therefore, actually projecting them onto another? Are you unwilling to admit that you are behaving badly, so you project it onto another? Before you can provide honest feedback to someone else, you must first be sure you're not simply looking into the mirror.

JOURNAL:

Creating or Revealing

Attempting to look or act a certain way in order to attract a partner is not the way to go. Working on improving aspects of yourself, though, is! Attempting to be something you are not in order to attract someone who is intrigued by what you are not becomes a living lie and gets progressively more painful. It is like throwing yourself in a prison to hide your true self. Stop that false representation!

When you feel good about yourself and love who you truly are, you become more attractive and confident in revealing true aspects of your self. You are spectacular if you truly allow yourself to be known. There is nothing advertisers can give you that will make you more wonderful than that which God bestows on you for your journey here on earth.

Reveal your magnificent beauty for all to see. How can you do that today?

JOURNAL:

Are You Ready For Love?

Many of us have hurts or failed relationships in our pasts. This can cause us to close down our hearts or shut our minds to the possibility of a relationship that works. If we are always waiting for the other shoe to drop or wondering when we will fail, then our intention is already setting us up for failure.

Making yourself ready for a relationship means opening yourself up, despite the past hurts and despite any mistrust or doubt you may have. Remembering that Spirit is your primary source, not a relationship, allows you to move forward with faith and confidence. Just as you are seeking a relationship, it is seeking you. Making yourself ready invites it in.

What do you need to let go of to make yourself ready for a relationship?

JOURNAL:

Be Who You Want to Be With

Are you the kind of person that you would want to be with? This is the most important question you can ask yourself in preparing for a relationship. Make a list of all the qualities you want in someone else. Affirm, visualize, and intend to be in relationship. Then, become the someone whom *that* someone would love.

Seeing yourself in relationship is opening your life to someone else. It is allowing the God-presence in through the eyes, heart, and mind of another, while knowing that they will be different than you are. It's celebrating the way two halves compliment each other, while creating a new whole that wasn't there before.

Imagine the relationship that you want to have. Then, spend some time writing about who you want to become in order to have that relationship.

JOURNAL:

The Power of Love

A story is told of a kindly bishop by the name of Valentine, who lived during a time when marriage was banned. He saw the pain it brought to lovers, so he secretly performed the sacrament of matrimony. It was only a matter of time before the Emperor Claudius II had Valentine, "Friend of Lovers," imprisoned.

It was believed that Valentine had the saintly power to heal. One day, his jailer brought his blind daughter to Valentine. Valentine helped his daughter, and the two began a wonderful friendship. When she heard he was to be executed, she went to his cell and found a farewell note to her signed, "From Your Valentine," a phrase that lives to this day. Some say his execution was on February 14, 270 AD.

This story is a reminder of the power of love, the *agape* love that transcends the physical. Agape brings a freedom from fear and a joy into imprisonment. It's a divine power that can make the blind see. To what have you been blinded that love could help you see? Take a moment to turn on your heart and look through loving energy at a difficult area in your life. See if your faith in love is strong enough to free you. Write about what that looks like.

JOURNAL:

Relationship as Spiritual Practice

What kind of relationship do you want to have? Can you imagine sharing your life, your home, your thoughts, and your heart with someone? What if they are not perfect? Relationship is one of the most challenging, yet rewarding, spiritual practices. Every rough edge you have is exposed, every old belief is questioned, and every area of control or neglect is revealed.

When you allow your relationship to be a spiritual practice, you engage in it with consciousness, intention, humility, and openness. Relationships invite you to become aware of family triggers and childhood hurts. They are constant reminders that it's never about someone else; it's always about the part you play. That's where healing is available.

What are you learning about yourself in your relationships?

JOURNAL:

Point of Transformation

One balmy morning, while sitting on the bluffs overlooking the beautiful Pacific Ocean, I saw a pod of dolphins swim by. I had always wanted to swim with the dolphins and thought this was my chance. As I ran into the ocean, however, I noticed my body freezing up with fear and my head questioning the wisdom of this action. My mind was quite convincing, pointing out that these were wild animals, far bigger than me, who could hold their breath a lot longer. This was water, not land. It was in this moment that I had to decide whether I was going to follow my logical mind—which was now making a lot of sense—or say "yes" to this opportunity of a heart's dream.

In the course of our lives, we come to a point of transformation where we must choose to follow our fear or follow our heart. You are the decision maker. No one else can tell you which direction to take. In my case, I chose to follow my heart. When I did, my body relaxed, and I could then hear the water filled with the sounds of playful dolphins, just like a Jacques Cousteau show. The dolphins surrounded me, we looked into each others' eyes, and now Flipper and I are the best of friends.

JOURNAL:

Loving Another

Opening your heart to loving another person offers a wonderful opportunity to see God in them. Each person is a unique, precious, radiant being of Light. When you see this in them, you help them see it in themselves. When you love someone, you help them know themselves as loveable.

Loving another person is a powerful recognition of their value, worth, and presence. As you love another, your intention for and attention to them grows and nurtures them.

How are the people in your life loveable? Write what you love about each special person in your life. How is your love a gift to them? What would it be like if you loved more openly, more deeply? What greater love could you bring to each person you love?

JOURNAL:

Friends and Family

You are surrounded by the love and presence of God. Sometimes it is a challenge to know and accept this. That's why God made friends and family. The people in your life who love you are manifestations of the love of God. Their hands are God's hands, lifting and supporting you. In their eyes, you see that God recognizes who you are.

Your friends and family also provide some of the best opportunities for you to express and experience God's unconditional love. Your love for them allows you the chance to feel unconditional Love as it pours out through you. The more you love, the more love you have, and the more love comes back to you. In this way, God's love and presence are multiplied.

How are your relationships with your friends and family? Is there anything that needs to be cleaned or opened up in order for more love to pour through?

JOURNAL:

They Know

From a bluff high above the beach, you can easily pick up the energy of the people strolling by far beneath you. Their etheric bodies are easy to sense when you have no attachment to or relationship with them. You can tell how they feel by objectively looking at their gait and posture. As you observe, notice the first awareness that comes into your conscious field. It doesn't matter if you are right or wrong—what you are doing is developing your deeper intuitive sense of connection. Since we are all connected, the possibility of knowing is ever present. If you really want to stretch your imaginative realm, try tapping into your dear friends to see if you can notice what's going on with them, even when they're not physically present.

Your body exposes your inner thoughts. As much as you may think you are fooling people, your posture, facial expression, tone of voice, eyes, body language, and every little move you make are windows to what's going on inside you. You may get so caught up in your self-expression that you forget what you are actually conveying. We are all connected; our bodies are just physiological expressions of our inner being.

Imagine someone really paying attention to your energetic field and sensing what was really going on with you. You'd be known!

JOURNAL:

Beyond Words

Have you wanted to tell a friend about your recent vacation, only to end up listening to your friend tell you all about their past vacations? It was as if they were only interested in their story to the exclusion of yours. It may have felt to you like oblivious one-upmanship. It wasn't about listening, hearing, or sharing; it was more like a competition. It is when personality isn't pushing and jockeying for position that you connect at a real, caring level with a true sense of support.

Have you ever controlled your words so another could feel safe to share with you? When you are with someone you care about, ask them questions, showing sincere interest and see how much deeper that takes you. Don't talk about how much you know or what you have seen. People enjoy talking about what they love, so give others a chance to feel your support. If there is silence in your dialogue, don't rush for words. Instead, connect with feeling. Your personality doesn't need to take charge. Be brave enough to simply look into the other person's eyes and see what is happening beyond words.

When were you uncomfortable in the silence with someone, yet stayed there long enough for the magic to happen, and what was that magic?

JOURNAL:

Tough Love

Sometimes the greatest love you can give to someone is to tell them the truth, instead of lying to be nice. Sometimes love is saying "no," rather than saying "yes" and creating resentment. Sometimes love is saying what you will and won't live with, accept, or tolerate.

Any of these actions creates a more mature, powerful love that honors both yourself and the one you love.

Are there other ways to give tough love? Are there any you should be using in your life?

JOURNAL:

Toxic Talk

Everyday, we teach people how to treat us. We give signals as to the acceptable way in which we are willing to engage in conversation and behavior. Our expressions and responses in any and every interaction reveal our self-worth and the vibration at which we are willing to play.

If we are willing to stay in the energetic field of exchange of someone who is verbally abusive or intimidating, then this person can no longer be the reason for the toxicity in your life. We become the ones who have chosen to remain in another's trash-talking environment. It takes two to argue. You can be the one to communicate from a higher place—which may look like walking away. Others can join you or remain in their own dump. But it's their choice, not yours.

Where in your life would you like to take the higher ground?

JOURNAL:

February 23
Don't Duke It Out

People say hurtful things, but the words only hurt if they find a receptive spot in your self-perspective. You can waste a lot of precious energy simmering about how other people view you and figuring out how you can get them to see you "correctly." Let their actions roll off you as if you were made of Teflon. What people see is actually a reflection of who they are, not who you are.

Don't duke it out with others. Spend your energy on yourself. It's a waste to lower yourself to another's vibration or frequency. Stop living someone else's version of you. Don't allow that which is most significant to you to become a victim of that which has no importance to you. Do yourself a favor and honestly examine who you are now, not what you were or what you used to be. Not even the people pleaser who put up the proper image is who you are today. Get current with yourself and get comfortable in your own skin. When you let people speculate about you without needing to convince them otherwise, you'll find an inner calm that you never knew existed.

JOURNAL:

The Energy of Love

When we have love going on, anything is possible. I'm not talking about a great date or a hot night in bed, but that soul-stirring, heart-opening surrender to the part which is connected to the Source. One doesn't get there through controlling situations or people, but by honoring the Divine spark. God is Love, and Love is the fuel.

You will attract more love into your life when you have greater self-respect. This kind of energy heightens your connectedness and makes you more attractive. A renewed passion and zest will reverberate back to you from everywhere. When you are in touch with this radiance, love gathers everything it desires into your world.

Where could you use love's energy in your life?

JOURNAL:

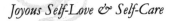

Loving Yourself

When you look at a child or an artist, isn't it easy to feel love? What about when you look at yourself in the mirror? Remember that you are also a child and an artist. You are whatever it is you love in another. If you don't possess the quality yourself, you couldn't love it in someone else. Focus on those qualities that you enjoy about yourself. Love them up! Focus on those things you wish were different. Love them, too. They're a part of what makes you who you are.

Loving yourself doesn't mean you stop growing and changing. It means that you see yourself with the same compassion and interest with which you see others.

Journal about those things you are now going to start loving in yourself. How does that make you feel?

JOURNAL:

It Can Move Mountains

More powerful than the waves of the ocean, the winds of the sky, or the shifting of the earth is Love. Love is the greatest avenue of Divine Expression that you can know. It can move mountains, transmute pain into joy, scarcity into abundance, and sickness into health. It will take the dim, dreary, down-and-out viewpoint on life and brighten the horizon with Infinite choices, enticing relationships, and fulfilling days.

What's keeping you from this exciting expression of God? Stop waiting around for someone else to deliver the goods. Get your love energy going today by writing yourself a Love Note. It all starts with loving yourself. Release your gift of love so that you will be uplifted, making you a more joyous and loving contributor to humanity.

JOURNAL:

Self-Care is Loving, Too

Are you so busy nurturing, caring for, and loving others that you have forgotten to give yourself those same gifts? It's challenging to give from an empty cup, so it's time to start making sure that your cup is also full.

Self-care comes in many forms—pampering, time alone, soft music, lunch dates, walks, sleep, and good food to name just a few. Loving yourself is simply another way that you allow Life to love Itself.

What kinds of self-care do you enjoy? How much of this self-care are you actually doing in your life? Do you need to add some more?

JOURNAL:

It's a Blessing

Your body is a great vehicle for you to travel this world in. It was meant to be enjoyed, not to make you feel bad. Spirit moves through your body. Why in the world would you want to deny your body its natural pleasures? God knew what It was doing when It shaped the body with all its accessories and put them together as you. The Law of Attraction isn't only for the birds and the bees or the metaphysical world. It also applies to the physical realm. Because you incarnated in this world, you might as well enjoy it while you are here—just so long as you don't bring anyone harm.

Making babies and making love are both divine acts. Who decided that one should be good and the other bad? And why would you accept other peoples' opinions on the matter when it feels so right? How could such a heavenly experience be considered wrong? Why would you think God is so uptight? Your body is a wonderful blessing and a gift, so you might as well enjoy it.

Do you have any attitudes that keep you from enjoying the physical act of love?

JOURNAL:

Step Off the Edge

The first card in a Tarot deck is the Holy Fool. On this card, a young man is shown stepping off the edge of a cliff. Displaying a complete lack of concern, he keeps his eyes on the horizon, instead of on the path before him. Some interpret the Holy Fool as naïve and unwise in the ways of the world. Yet, he is protected by his innocence and complete trust.

There is a saying: "When you step off the edge of all you know, into the unknown, one of two things will happen: You will either find solid ground, or you will learn to fly." Invite the archetype of the Holy Fool to help you leap into the unknown, with perfect trust in Spirit.

What are you holding on to? What are you afraid of? Journal about moving through your life with greater trust and complete innocence.

JOURNAL:

FREE TO CHOOSE

March 1-9
Joyously Springing into Life

March 10-23
The Joy of Choosing What to Think (& Not to Think)

March 24-30
Joyous Spiritual Practices

Put a Spring in Your Step

Your life is a gift to be enjoyed. Your very being is a gift to the world. Your smile spreads love, your joy spreads happiness, and your positive outlook lifts situations and people all around you.

Allow this truth to seep into your soul. You are part of the universe; you have a right to be here. Let this truth light your path, lift your heart, and put a spring in your step.

JOURNAL:

Enjoying Newness

Spring is a wonderful time of new beginnings, new life, and new growth. You are invited into the spring of your own life. What is new?

If there isn't anything new right now, create spring in your life. Create something new. Make space for something new, or decide something new. What do you want to be new in your life?

JOURNAL:

A New Day

As you awaken to the morning, moving from the dream state to the conscious world, do you become aware of the new day and the wonderful possibilities before you? Do you say, "Good morning, God!" or "Good God, it's morning!"? The mental thoughts you wake up with can set the tone for what comes to you the rest of the day. When thrust forth into your day, how you embrace the choices at hand determines the kinds of experiences you'll encounter.

Life holds multiple opportunities to start anew. An unwanted breakup, a sudden death, a surprise job ending, or a devastating illness can be shocking awakenings from your previous state of being. But no matter what happens, you are still at choice as to how you greet the new day.

What was your experience when you chose to embrace a challenge rather than resist it?

JOURNAL:

New Life Stirs Within

Become aware as new ideas, a new inner urging, and a renewed sense of purpose arise within you. Seek to feel the ways new life constantly stirs within you. Spirit is always seeking to express more of Itself as you—more life, more love, more joy—and your life is ever growing to accommodate this inner urge.

Sometimes, new life stirs up and reawakens an old sense of purpose. This may be something you put away as childish, silly, or unattainable. Sometimes, life stirs by prompting something so new you've never considered it before. This may also feel silly or unattainable.

Listen for and write about these inner urgings. How is new life stirring within you today? If you stopped thinking it was silly or unattainable, what new thing would you start growing in your life?

JOURNAL:

Transcend Human Knowing

Stop carrying your burdens to God. You do not need to describe your pains to Spirit in graphic detail. It's ridiculous to think Spirit created us and then dumped us because we messed up somewhere. You struggle because you have dumped God in favor of your burden! You have forgotten the touch of God. Don't go asking for healing. Stop complaining about what's wrong and throw away your litany of ailments.

Very simply, drop your burdens. Turn within and allow the heavenly Presence to be remembered and revealed. As the Divine is revealed, something happens in your field of awareness that allows guidance, protection, and wisdom to take over. An understanding that transcends human knowing becomes the vision through which you see.

Where in your life would you like a new vision?

JOURNAL:

Expect Great Things

The bird stands ready at the edge of the nest. Never having spread its wings before, it still expects to fly! You stand at the edge of your life. Perhaps your past has not been everything you would have liked it to be. You can, however, still expect great things.

You were meant to be all that you can be, because you are the very incarnation of Spirit as you. Right now, just as you are, this is already true, even if you've not experienced it before. Stand at the edge of your life, spread your spiritual truths, and expect great things!

JOURNAL:

Expanding Reality

There can be advantages to walking on the edge. What you see from there is far greater than what is seen by those who play it safe, staying back and embracing the collective perspective of what's "out there." Fringe dwellers have the ability to see both sides of an equation. They can live between two worlds, having the ability to choose their reality. Where are you tired and stuck perceiving reality in a non-supportive way? What reality would you like to expand into your world?

Catch the natural currents. Though they may be invisible to the human eye, they are still there, waiting to lift you to a greater panoramic view with greater choices. Just as the eagle effortlessly soars on invisible mountain currents in the sky, so you, too, can be lifted. The higher you go, the less attached you become to the particulars of the present realities that have you pinned down. Let go. Ride the celestial winds of Spirit, and let them take you where you are intended to be and reveal what you are intended to see.

JOURNAL:

Staying with Your Intention

How do you stay focused on your intention while waiting for it to become real in your life? This is perhaps one of the hardest aspects of spiritual living. The best analogy I know is the seed in the garden. When you plant a carrot seed, for instance, you do so because you want carrots. You expect carrots, and you assume you will grow carrots from the carrot seeds. You know what will grow even before you see any little leaves poking out through the soil. Even then, it's still weeks before you can pick the fully-grown carrots.

The same is true with your intention. Once you have set your intention, you must stay focused on the end result. Even when you can't see anything happening, you must know it is. Once little things start happening along the way, you know it may still be some time before your intention is fully grown. Be patient, stay focused, and remember the carrot.

JOURNAL:

Busting into Bloom

Before the trees pop into bloom in the spring, you can see and feel the accumulating energy rising in and filling each one of the buds to the point where they have no choice but to burst forth into expression. What a powerful lesson—to allow the energy to rise within until you are not only compelled to take action, but you have the strength to break through whatever has been holding you back.

Just as a tree's roots gain nurturance from the soil, so do you gain the energy to blossom in your world as you keep your mind stayed on Spirit. Resistance to bringing forth your innate gifts gives way to entertaining the Divine. You lack nothing when you are one with God. Continue to seek Spirit, not something *from* Spirit. Only then will you have accumulated energy within that will beautifully burst forth in your garden of life at the perfect time.

Where could you gather more energy before proceeding with a project?

JOURNAL:

Predestined

How wonderful it is to have choice! There is nothing set in stone that is destined to happen to you. You set patterns into motion that become joyous revelations or constrictive entrapments, but this is the natural unfolding of your actions. It is not predestiny, but the inevitable outcome of the Law in action. You can step away from your creations anytime you chose to set a new cause into motion. It might take time to extricate yourself from the present patterns and consequences you've created, but you must remember that you can.

Are you ready to assume the obligation for your life? Your responsibility lies not only in your readiness, but in a willingness to live a new expression of your being. With what new level of your true identity are your ready to identify? In what areas of your life would you like to be free? How can you set a new cause into motion?

JOURNAL:

You Have Preferences

Have you ever asked a friend what he wanted for dinner, only to have him say, "I don't care. You decide. I'm not attached." It's as if he was practicing some great spiritual principle of non-attachment. Try taking him to a fish house when he can't stand fish and you just might find some attachment!

Having preferences in life is fine. When someone asks what movie would you like to see, be bold and speak up, rather than say it doesn't matter when it does. If you don't like violent, slasher flicks, then seeing "Exterminator 67" matters!

As the creator of your life, you get to choose which color you surround yourself with. If you like bright, vivid, Caribbean colors, you can have them. You don't have to settle for the muted tones. Some things matter more than others, like a long-time marriage coming to an end or a cup of coffee being empty. If your coffee carries as much significance as your relationship, you might want to re-evaluate your preference list.

Where in your life do you say it doesn't matter when it really does?

JOURNAL:

Trusting the Law

Every spiritual tradition teaches the power of prayer. This power is actually the power of the Universal Spiritual Law that co-creates life through your belief and intention. Jesus of Nazareth taught this law when he said, "As you believe, so be it done unto you." Your only focus needs to be on your thoughts and beliefs. The Law will take care of the rest.

This is an amazing place of hope and comfort. You don't have to figure out how something will heal or be manifested. All you need to do is trust in the Law. You use this trust every time you plant a seed. You trust that the seed and the soil, through some process no one really understands, will grow into the plant you intend. Trust the Law with your intention and belief, and it will grow into what you desire.

JOURNAL:

The Power of Your Thought

Pay attention to the thoughts that you think—not those that have the most energy, intention, or repetition—because the thoughts you think are creating your life.

You might ask yourself what you spend the most time thinking about. (Repetition.) You might focus on what thoughts cause your heart to race or your stomach to churn. (Energy.) You may also want to focus on which thoughts you deliberately think—in a concentrated, concerted manner—because you have decided to choose to think about them. (Intention.)

Your trained thought, which you use in affirmations, affirmative prayer, or any intentional work in consciousness, is much more powerful than any thought you randomly think. When this deliberate thought is coupled with the energy of conviction or intention, it's unstoppable.

Journal about how much trained thought you are using every day.

JOURNAL:

You Choose What to Plant

You are completely free to plant whatever you want to grow in the garden of your life. Are you making that choice consciously, or are you simply letting things grow out of habit?

Are you planting weeds that will choke out your garden through ongoing negativity, judgment, criticism, complaint, unforgiveness, or fear? Or, are you planting seeds that will bloom and bear fruit through deliberate and conscious attention to the good in your life, the joy you experience, the abundance that is yours, and the presence of Spirit and Love that is real?

Your intention is what plants the seed. Your *attention* is what makes it grow. Around what are you choosing to have intention, and to what are you paying attention?

JOURNAL:

Stinking Thinking

Wherever John went during the past two days, everything seemed to stink badly, and people seemed to be avoiding him. Then one night, when he was taking off his sneakers, he realized he had stepped in dog poop. He was the one bringing the smell with him.

Most of our thoughts are reruns, just following us around. No one can stink up your world as much as you can with your negative thoughts, and no one can refresh and beautify your world as much as you can with your positive ones. Your world is created by either your stinking thinking or your clear thinking. Don't get caught filling your world with an odious odor or messing up your experience with repulsive thoughts.

Where can you use a little refreshing in your world?

JOURNAL:

Who Decides?

When you watch your child in a sporting event, you might be anxious about your child's performance. Another parent watching your child would be experiencing the same thing but with less emotional attachment than you. And the referee orchestrating the game has an entirely different kind of experience of that same event.

It's important to realize that you bring an energetic charge to every situation that colors your perspective and determines your experience. Who decides what colors, filters, or emotions you will use to perceive an event? You empower your life by making a conscious choice of where you want to engage. You don't need to give this power away to external happenings. Life, with its highs and lows, is fun when you realize you get to choose the situations to which you will devote yourself. Your energy and time are too precious to give away to jerks, dumb moves, and unconscious individuals. Make sure you consciously decide your relationship to any of the happenings in your life.

Where in your life would it be good to take back the energy that you previously gave away?

JOURNAL:

Hypothetical Non-happenings

I entered the rental car agency on the Sunday evening of a holiday week. The counter people were exhausted and out of SUVs, the model I had reserved months prior. They gave me a small car for my snowy mountainous experience. The sign at the counter invited me to check to see if the car was in good condition. I went outside into below-20 degree weather, did a quick walk around, found no dings, and drove off.

The next day, walking up to the car in the sunlight, I noticed that the spoiler underneath the front bumper was smashed. A few days prior to returning the car, my concern of being held responsible for what I had not done began to weigh on me. I'd even go to sleep thinking about how much I was going to get charged for it. When the day arrived to return the car, the check-in person was as nice as could be and couldn't have cared less about the damaged spoiler.

How often have you worried and stressed over something that never came to pass? When have you wasted your precious energy and mindspace on a hypothetical non-happening? Imagine being fully present and enjoying the moment you are in, dealing with the challenges only when it's time to deal with them. Or, you can worry in advance and miss the good that is all around you!

JOURNAL:

Don't Dig Up the Seed

Can you imagine what would happen if you planted a row of seeds and then kept digging them up to see if they were growing? How can the seed keep maturing its little roots and drawing what it needs from the soil if you keep pulling it out to see if it's growing? Can you see how the seed would have to start over again each time, putting out new, little root hairs? At some point, it will simply not be able to do that, at which point the seed will no longer grow.

You dig up your seed every time you doubt something, fear it won't happen, interfere by trying to make it happen yourself, or simply fret and worry about it.

Journal about the following question: In what ways are you digging up your seeds of intentional, affirmative thought?

JOURNAL:

Plowing Through

Plowing your way through a challenge with your head down and no concern for where you end up or the damage you cause is not necessarily the best way to work through conflict. Wherever you find yourself in life, you have the opportunity to grow, to bring forth Spirit, and to reveal your true character. You are always given the opportunity to emerge from adversity stronger than when you entered it.

Taking advantage of opportunity calls on your ability to understand your vision instead of the impending doom. In this three-dimensional world, there are opposing energies attempting to win. In the spiritual realm, which is the Truth of you, there are no conflicting energies. So, move from the human mind to Divine Consciousness, where there is only Spirit—not Spirit overcoming anything, but only Spirit. Stop praying to heal the challenge or to have God do something for you. Stop seeking, and try resting in God, allowing the higher vision to emerge as the way on your path and through this physical world's challenges.

JOURNAL:

Allowing Things to Grow

You've planted your seeds and watered your garden. Now what do you do? You wait for things to grow. There is an inherent Law of Growth in each seed which already knows what is needed to become a full, healthy plant bearing fruit and flower. Once the seed is planted, after we water and fertilize it, our job is to let it grow.

How true is this in your life? Are you allowing things to grow in their own time, in their own way? Where are you becoming impatient and, therefore, doubtful? Spend some time imagining the things you've intended for your life growing all on their own. What if you simply relaxed and allowed that growth to happen? How does that feel? What do you do while you're allowing things to grow?

JOURNAL:

Weeding Your Mind

Once again, you find yourself feeling the same doubts, the same anger, or the same unpleasant feelings you've felt before. And, once again, they feel true and real. Where do these feelings come from? They are a product of thoughts and beliefs that grow as weeds in the garden of your mind: weeds of doubting yourself, because of something that happened to you in Junior High; weeds of inadequacy, because of things your parents said to you; weeds of anger, because your family constantly fought. However these weeds were planted, they are bearing fruit that is no longer what you choose to have in your life.

Ask yourself, "When have I felt this feeling before? When was the first time I felt it? How is this feeling being re-created over and over again in my life? What do I choose to believe instead? What do I know is my spiritual truth?"

JOURNAL:

Chaos and Crashes

During recessions and depressions, we hear stories of people taking their lives because of the disappearance of their earthly wealth. People can get so caught up with form that when it's not there, they think it is gone. Yet, it's not as if the government has stopped printing money. In fact, it seems to be printing more! The Divine Intelligence that created wealth and has time and time again risen above the repressed ways of this world, has manifested a wealthy way of being after every depression so far. God is not going to let the world it created stay down for too long. "This too shall pass" was the wisdom given to Solomon. One does not live by bread alone or by what has already been created.

If the whole world were to disappear tomorrow, those who know that-which-is-seen comes from that-which-is-not seen, or that the invisible passes into form through conscious awareness, will once again have Good in their world. When you have the courage to face the disillusionment of this world with the knowledge of the Infinite, you find a whole new world springing up out of chaos and crashes. The same wisdom that created your original Good will do it again and again and again. You are the key and the channel to God made manifest. You do not live on what was, but by every word that comes forth from your mouth and every thought you entertain.

What thoughts do you want to dump and which new ones do you want to entertain?

JOURNAL:

Untying the Knot

Untying a knot takes tenacity and patience. How such a mess can be made so quickly is one of life's mysteries! To straighten it out requires loosening the tension and methodically moving through each tangle of the knot one at a time, not giving in to the frustration until it's untangled.

Sometimes, it's a mystery as to how your life has gotten all tangled, tightened, and stuck in a big, old knot. Relaxing and loosening up as much as possible on one element of the entanglement is a start. That clearing will naturally lead to the next piece of the puzzle to be worked on. Working at extricating yourself from each small, puzzling twist and tie makes the next situation more manageable, eventually leading to a clear path for creating your life from choice. It takes sticking to the process and utilizing your innate strengths and abilities to move through each small aspect until the whole knot has been undone.

Any knots in your life you'd like to start untying? Where should you start?

JOURNAL:

More Important than God?

As Gandhi was leading an amazing transformation in India from British rule to self rule, one can only imagine the demand on his time for leadership. Yet, no matter how hectic things were or how urgently his attention was needed on certain matters, he saved one day a week for silence. It didn't matter how pressing the issues, Gandhi kept inviolate his time with his Higher Power. He knew that only when he was connected with a greater wisdom could he make the wise decisions before him.

If you can't clear a full day a week, can you reserve a specific time in the course of your day, keeping it uninterrupted by the pressing issues of your world? Do you make your time with God a high priority, or does it get relegated to a lower spot on your to-do list? Do you refuse to entertain demands for attention during your regularly scheduled sacred time? What do you feel is so much more important than God that it would get your time and attention instead?

JOURNAL:

Tending Your Garden

Every day you tend your life by tending to the garden of your mind and consciousness. Planting, weeding, mulching, fertilizing, watering, and pruning all have a place in this process. Preparing the soil, choosing the seeds, thinning rows, transplanting, and harvesting are also required.

How can you relate this analogy to the things you do in your mind and consciousness to tend to your life? What are you planting? When are you weeding? Why would you mulch? What are you using as fertilizer? What needs to be pruned?

Spend some time exploring these ideas, and see what you are doing well and where more attention might be needed.

JOURNAL:

Devotions No Matter What

When you are devoted to your spiritual practices, you sometimes do your readings or quiet your mind simply out of commitment. Other times, though, you do it out of joy, upliftment, and revitalization. Devotion can seem like a chore, but it is best to be consistent in connecting with Source, particularly when your environment is not your normal, peaceful abode.

Within yourself is the strength to persevere with your spiritual work. Outside are the reasons you don't have time, or the place is not right, or the other demands are seemingly more important than experiencing God.

How can you make a consistent space in your waking hours to practice your devotions every day—no matter what?

JOURNAL:

Cultivating Your Soil

Your consciousness is the soil in which your intentions take root and grow. Is your consciousness rich and fertile, receiving your intentions easily and helping them grow? Or is your consciousness hard and closed, rejecting new intentions? Or is it dry and barren, with nothing to give in support of your new life?

You can cultivate a rich and fertile consciousness every day. This might include tilling the soil with daily spiritual practices, providing the sunshine of a positive outlook, fertilizing with a willingness to see things differently, watering with possibilities, and allowing Life to grow you.

Are you open to cultivating the soil of your life? What are you currently doing to grow your consciousness?

JOURNAL:

Good Morning

How you start the day has a lot to do with how you experience it. If you start off rushed, you'll probably be racing throughout your day. If you begin with a bad attitude, you will attract reasons to be in a foul mood. If your morning includes meditation—taking some time to be with God, remembering your Source—you'll approach everything life throws at you this day with a calm, trusting response. You'll see Spirit showing up everywhere.

Throughout the day you are given the choice: to respond from love or from something else. The dominant voice that will play in your head is often speaking before you leave the house. How can you be in a good place when upsetting thoughts fill your field of awareness? Yet, you can make a difference, bringing love to where it's missing.

How are you going to start your day?

JOURNAL:

Listen to Your Prayers Speak

I have a dog and a cat who believe their days start at the first light of dawn. My wife, on the other hand, doesn't have the same philosophy. Yet, she supports their position by having me escort them and their energetic greeting of the day away from the bedroom. Since there is no other activity around our house at that hour, I feed Zac, the cat, and take Sage, the dog, for a walk. As I stroll along, I notice how quiet my thoughts are at this time of morning. My thoughts aren't involved with how to fix or heal anything. They are focused on the spectacular sunrise or the beauty of the day and seeing a God Presence everywhere I look.

My prayer work that time of morning is not about overcoming or improving any of the situations on my list of prayer requests. What I witness is the consciousness that brings these to my awareness giving way to listening only to God. That which I had been seeking, I am. In that quiet moment, there is no other mind than the Mind of the Divine. It embodies every quality and activity necessary, not from a correcting place, but from the awareness that there is no perspective other than God's.

Rather than speaking your prayers, try to get up a little early and listen to your prayers speaking through you.

JOURNAL:

Dawn Patrol

When the nine-to-five routine doesn't give you the freedom to do your spiritual work, try the dawn patrol approach and go five-to nine. In the skiing, surfing, and physical fitness communities, some of the best experiences happen before most people have had their breakfast. This time of connection gives you more energy to deal with the "cubical farm" of the workplace.

Of course, everything in your day can be a spiritual expression. To begin your day with this kind of activity and heightened awareness, though, will permeate your interactions for the remaining twenty hours. You must have some dedicated spiritual or contemplative consciousness in your day. Opening the Divine circuits within yourself prepares you to embrace God in everything you do and in every way you do it. Living in Spirit does not manifest by doing nothing. It is brought forth in your activities, and there is a lot more fun in an activity that you love. It will raise your energy level for the rest of the day.

What practice would get you out of bed earlier?

JOURNAL:

Planting Seeds of a New Life

Everyday you have the opportunity to think a new thought. This new thought is a seed of the new life you want to create and experience. Plant this thought in your consciousness as if you were planting a row of carrot seeds. Each time you affirm this idea, imagine you are planting another seed in the row.

What new thought do you want to plant today? Take some time to write down some of the things you'd like to become or experience. Then, imagine what new thought embodies that idea. You might start with, "I now think…" As you write this down, feel what resonates with you the most in this moment. Begin today planting that new thought, over and over and over again.

JOURNAL:

Joy of Rebirth

April 1-6
Freedom of the Christ Consciousness

April 7-16
Freedom from the Tomb

April 17-24
The Freedom of Forgiveness

April 25-30
A Free & Open Consciousness

Trust in the Light

The Light of Life is shining in and through your life, right now. You don't have to be any more spiritual than you are today, or anymore together, or anymore whatever it is you think needs to be fixed about you. You are already the incarnation of the One Life, as you. You are already a bearer of Light, a bringer of Peace, and a vessel of Love. All you have to do is remember this truth and trust in the Light that you are.

JOURNAL:

Beyond Belief

Polls show a great majority of people believe in God. It is truly mind boggling the way the earth and planets—within a universe or a galaxy—move around the sun with such perfection that they can be charted out millions of years forward and backward to the very second of their locations. Who could deny some type of order and Infinite Intelligence is behind all this?

But there must be more than a belief in a higher power; there must be the experience of it. It must be real for you. Behind all these effects there must be a cause. When you come to the realization that there is a first cause and it initiates the impulse of your world, you become the beneficiary to God's Grace.

How can you move beyond belief to become the embodiment of the Divine?

JOURNAL:

Beyond the Surface

Scuba diving on a wild and windy day when the seas are breaking over the front of the boat can make you wonder, "What am I doing out here?" Yet when you jump into the ocean, what you then experience— the calm, quiet, and magical gifts of the deeper dimension— makes it all worth it. For Spirit to be heard and seen, you need to leave the chatter and confusion behind you.

When your world is wild, crazy, and turbulent, you can find an unfathomable place that has not been disturbed by unstable, chaotic experiences. It's waiting for you to stop bobbing about, cease the flailing to stay afloat, and dive beneath the surface of your life. There is something in the deep nature of your being that waits to be discovered. Then, when you return to the surface, you find a renewed passion and excitement. Having seen what others haven't yet seen gives you a different kind of strength to navigate through the world.

What's in the deeper aspect of your being that is waiting to be discovered?

JOURNAL:

Richness of True Identity

Are you spending too much time with unnecessary things? Do you find yourself involved in daily activities that don't really excite your soul? When you allow other peoples' thoughts to enter your mind space, you can lose touch with the rhythm of being. You must know there is another way. The realization that you are doing something that isn't working anymore, and your willingness to do something about it, creates space for the higher vibration of your true Self to be felt again.

Life is looking for you to grow through love and joy. When you don't act with love and joy, pain and shock become your lessons. Regardless, you will grow. You play in the world of your choosing. You have an individual expression that removes you from the world of competition. It reveals your inner nature. You were individually conceived and born in love, created with unique gifts and talents to share. There is no way to hold back the reservoir of riches that will come your way when you share your true identity with the world.

In what part of your life are you holding back your true Self?

JOURNAL:

The Christ Realization

How many prostitutes and blind or sick people did Jesus meet on his path? None! He always saw the Christ expression in each person he met. No matter what the story, the diagnosis, or prognosis, he saw Wholeness. This is the key to healing: to see as God sees and to know there is no otherness. One must know there is no power, disease, lack, or limitation to overcome. There is but One Power, One Presence, and this is God.

You can throw off the influences of the world by showing forth the grace of the Divine at any time, no matter how messed up things have become in your earthly experience. When you stop trying to demonstrate a supremacy over things and just demonstrate a consciousness of the God Presence, then, like Jesus, you'll call forth the Christ qualities. You are being called upon at this time to know the Truth and contemplate Spirit's Presence when others can't. All solutions are the realization of God within the moment. You have been chosen to know this!

Where in your life can you use a bit more knowing of the Christ realization?

JOURNAL:

Lost in the Wrong World

Have you ever been lost in thought and then jolted back to reality by a loud noise or sudden event? Have you ever been so identified with your story, when suddenly some event rocked your world and it fell away? Occasionally in life, people enter a transcendent state where the line between "I" and "others" blurs. This opening to the mystical domain of selfless light and rapture gives you insight into the flow of creation, where all struggle disappears.

It's easy to get lost in this world of form and phenomenon that you walk around in, believing it is your true identity. Yet, far greater harmonizing energies can overshadow your bodily world. Awaken, startled or gently, from the nightmare of false identification. In the new awareness of Oneness, all Good can be yours by Grace, without taking it from anyone or anything. The touch of God opens your spiritual centers. Illumination is yours, and the divided departmentalization of mind dissolves.

JOURNAL:

Dark Night of the Soul

Teachers have told tales of it and philosophers have written about it, but the only way to really know it yourself is to find your own way through the Dark Night of the Soul. There comes a point in life when nothing makes sense and you are brought to your knees in soul-felt surrender to your higher power. You don't know where to turn, the inner voice is silent, your life force has evaporated. You don't know how to go on. It's a disturbing time, a lonely time, when your cries for direction don't seem to be answered.

Though doubt seems to lead your life, this is a time of deep trust. It's an era of waiting, introspection, and patience, an occasion to review, reflect, re-evaluate, and re-invent yourself. You must learn to let go. You must go within to heal, forgive, and wait for the higher wisdom to emerge from the ashes. As much as you want out, don't rush this natural cycle of burning away your old self. This, too, shall pass. Don't give in to disbelief. Prove your trust is greater, and the gifts of this time will be immeasurable for your soul's growth.

JOURNAL:

Dark Nights of Unknowing

Everyone has moments, days, weeks, and sometimes even months of being depressed and uncertain. These are the quiet, fallow times of life, the darkness of winter before the burst of spring. While you may be uncomfortable during these times, it is important to remember that they, too, have their place.

Think of it like the cool, damp, rich darkness of the soil into which the seed is planted. For days, it doesn't look like anything is happening above ground. But underneath, that seed is germinating. Soon it puts out root hairs, and then a tender, little stalk reaching for the sun. This is a quiet, precious time of waiting, in awe, with faith, knowing that something *is* actually happening.

What is happening in your dark night? What is waiting in the dark for your Spring?

JOURNAL:

Tomb or Womb

When one is personality driven, simple truths can be difficult to hear. If your world caves in, it might actually be a blessing. As you lie entombed in the rubble of your own making, you get to decide whether you are in a tomb or a womb. It would have been a good thing to have not been buried alive, of course. Simple humility might have helped you see the collapse coming. But if you don't learn from the cave-ins of your life, you'll remain trapped in your false entitlements.

By taking a bold and honest look at the behavior that brought you to this place, you can realize the possibility of coming out alive as a new person. When you surrender the anxiety-filled entitlement of how you think the world should respond to you, you'll find the load lightens. If you use the time of darkness for introspection, it can become the regenerative womb for your soul's growth. Letting go of the me-centered approach to life and turning your trust over to your higher power, you can see that the collapse was a valuable learning experience, the birth to a new life.

When has your world slowed you down enough to birth a new aspect of your life?

JOURNAL:

The Narrow Passages

Passing through a difficult time is like an initiation. As you go through the narrow passages of the trial and move deeper into the uncharted aspects of your being, a new kind of trust emerges. You will be guided through the unknown, but you'll only come to know this by having gone there. You are forced to shift your sense of self and grow beyond your fears into a new kind of wisdom.

Your outer world may not instantly change, but something will have happened inside you. You will have a new level of freedom, compassion, and rebirth, because you have entered the space between the worlds of the known and unknown. Death loses its grip, your heart expands, and you have a full aliveness like never before. Reunion with your higher self is a gift that will weave its expression through all aspects of your life, freeing you from all limitations and conflicts.

What did you learn about yourself from past initiations?

JOURNAL:

Self Dying to Self

The ego (self) is a powerful and useful part of you that helps you negotiate and live in the world of physical form. It develops strategies for survival, coping mechanisms, and a whole system of categorizing that helps you understand the world and your place in it.

The problem is that these skills do not help you experience your Oneness or help you know your Spiritual Self and Authentically True Reality. Experiencing Oneness means you let go of your categories and separations. Knowing Reality, in the mystical sense, shows you Life beyond the physical world.

This experience invites the self to let go, so the Self can be revealed. Are you ready?

JOURNAL:

Claiming Good from Pain

Life doesn't always unfold just as we think it should. Sometimes painful things happen. People die, loved ones leave, jobs disappear, or you don't get something you really wanted. Spiritual maturity does not keep us from feeling the pain of these moments. Instead, it teaches us how to walk through them as gracefully as we can and not to stay stuck in our pain for too long.

One thing you can do in the midst of pain is declare that good must come of it. You don't need to know what that good is. You don't even need to know when the good will come. When you simply declare that good will come of it, the Universal Law will have to make good of it.

This does not mean that painful experiences are good. Nor does it mean that you have to experience pain to acquire good. It simply means that good can come from even the most painful things. So, you declare that to be so and expect it. This keeps you from wallowing in victimhood or despair.

JOURNAL:

Rising Again

The phoenix dies in ashes, from which it will rise again. The maize-corn god was buried in the ground for three days. From this site, maize grew, allowing the god to rise again. Jesus was crucified, buried, and rose again. In so many spiritual stories, we see a reminder that life always rises again.

What part of your life is in ashes today? Journal about the times when you have risen from the ashes of your life. Remind yourself what good came of those experiences. Can you sense what might be rising out of the ashes of today?

JOURNAL:

Knowing Life Never ends

The same Life that is the heartbeat of the Universe is at the center of all Life everywhere. Your life, all Life, is One Life. This body in which you are clothed is simply the earthly spacesuit Life requires to manage this plane of existence as you. When this spacesuit wears out, you will simply lay it down and move on to the next adventure Life has in store *as* you.

Since this is true for you, this is true for everyone and all beings everywhere. No Life can be lost. No Life can end. It simply changes form and enters into a new expression.

JOURNAL:

April 15
Moving On

Explaining the death of a beloved grandparent to a child can simplify and clarify your own understanding of the transition from this world to the next. Death is a time of soul-searching honesty. It is as natural and common as birth. The transition is as nurtured as that of coming into this world. It's fine to let the child know that Grandpa's body wasn't working well anymore and that, at a certain point, Grandpa let go of it. But explaining that Grandpa is in some mythical heavenly place will only deny the child the last gift Grandpa has given him or her. Grandpa, who made those eyes twinkle, is moving on ahead.

Just as you received an appropriate body for your spirit's journey on this Earth, you'll get the appropriate vehicle to move your awareness after you leave this plane. Just as love brought your family together on this plane, love will transcend time and space to keep us all together over many lifetimes. Grandpa has gone ahead to show us the way and make our arrival a bit easier. Now you know an ancestor on the other side who will be there to guide and protect you as you walk through this world.

How would you communicate your understanding of death to a child?

JOURNAL:

Birth and Rebirth

To be born again is to start fresh with the innocence of a child, the ability to wonder at life, filled with awe at all the amazingly good and wonderful things there are.

Each day is a new beginning. Every moment is a new start. What new way of being, seeing, and living is being born in you?

JOURNAL:

Releasing the Old

To create something new in your life, you have to make space by releasing the old. Often, the old is very comfortable; it's familiar and has already been broken in. Often, you don't even realize how much you are holding on to, because you think that's as good as it gets, or you don't deserve any better, or maybe there won't be anymore, so you'd better stick with what you have.

One of the spiritual truths, however, is that the Universe expands by constantly outgrowing the circle it is in. Think of the discarded shell of a crab, a river as it overflows its banks to fertilize the fields, or a creeping forest that overtakes an abandoned field. In every case, something new and more alive is created.

What angels, comfortable ruts, or old ways do you need to release in order for the beautiful and magnificent you to emerge?

JOURNAL:

Got to Leave it Behind

My Golden Retriever once found a fallen tree branch in the backyard. He grabbed one end of the branch and dragged it around all afternoon like he was the luckiest dog in the neighborhood. He was so proud. But when it was time to come inside for the evening, he couldn't get the branch through his doggy door. He pulled it, pushed it, and even maneuvered it sideways, but no matter how hard he tried, he couldn't get it through.

When it's time for us to leave this world behind, we can't take it with us, no matter how hard we try. You have traveled through this dimension of experience achieving and accumulating great things, and you have the plaques to prove it. But when it's time to return to that Divine place from whence you came, all your stuff has to be left outside. You must return as unencumbered as when you arrived.

Are there any branches you've been dragging around that you could release now?

JOURNAL:

Treasured Wounds

Life would be filled with a lot more joy if you simply agreed with God instead of resisting the Divine Vision for your life. The more you live in agreement, as opposed to resistance, the more wonderful life is. Treasured wounds hinder you and don't make sense for a person who wants freedom. You know the wounds I speak of; they are the ones you are still talking about. How was your world changed when you were wronged in the past? You have every little detail down, because you have thought about it incessantly into the late night/early morning hours and then described it throughout the day to people who really don't care.

If you want freedom and joy back in your life, you have to let go of the past. Divine harmony can return to your life only in proportion to the space you give it when you allow God back into your heart. If there is no room because your mind has become fixated and taken over by rehashing the treasured wounds, then you've locked out God. You must sit yourself down, and start contemplating and meditating on the nature of God. Let this renewed awareness fill your mind and heart, leading you to your healing, and revealing your true nature.

What treasured wounds are you rehashing, and what are they attempting to tell you?

JOURNAL:

Letting Go of the Past

The past holds two seductive challenges for you. It houses memories of the "good old days"—those days of youth, fun times, or special moments that keep you yearning to recreate them. It also holds memories that fester and smolder with anger or unforgiveness—those moments of "I can't believe that happened"—into which your thoughts keep getting trapped.

Focusing on these things from the past is like moving through life while looking in the rearview mirror.

To what part of your past are you clinging? Journal about what you need to do to let it go. Forgive? Release? Find joy in the here and now?

JOURNAL:

Forgiveness is a Choice

In forgiveness, you must face the hurt and disillusionment of deceit. What is it that closed down your heart? Are you ready to free the part of you that is held hostage and is still caught in the past? Are you ready to open up again? Are you willing to let go of the pain of the past—or do you still want it? When you stop arduously dragging what was originally no good into your future, you'll feel a lot better.

Reconnecting with life is what forgiveness is all about. It's a choice. Let go, even if it's only for selfish reasons. Forgiveness frees you from the stranglehold of the past. It releases you from the burden of pain and anger, so that you may be present for life now. It doesn't mean agreeing with what took place. It means allowing your soul to be free again to fully embrace the beauty and joy of life.

Write about a time you forgave a situation and how much better you felt afterward. Are there any areas in which you'd like to experience that feeling now?

JOURNAL:

Earth Day

Allow today to inspire your appreciation for this awesome and wonderful organism you live on called Earth. Take time today to become aware of some of the environmental issues currently taking place on your planet. You can pretend there aren't any, or you can choose to make yourself aware of them now.

You don't need to get radical and go on a rampage to change the way others do things, unless that's your personality. It is through awareness that you make a difference to everyone. Awareness can lead to healing in your physical body, and awareness can also lead to healing when it comes to the planetary body. When you don't know better, you can't act better. So, do yourself a favor and find out what's happening in your home. You may find a simple thing or two you can do to make a difference, and you'll notice how good you feel about your contribution.

What are some of the challenging environmental issues taking place on the planet that surprise you? What are a couple of things you can do differently to lessen your impact on the environment?

JOURNAL:

Forgive Them

How much space do you rent out in your mind and in your heart to people and events from the past? People and events are able to rent this space through your unforgiveness. All the time and energy you spend thinking about and brooding upon these events is time and energy that is not available for your greater good. As long as that space is rented out, it is unavailable for love, creativity, joy, or Spirit.

Forgiveness doesn't mean forgetting what happened; it means that you don't keep re-living it, wishing it were different, and being mad that it isn't. Forgiveness means accepting what is and letting it be. In the process, enormous amounts of time and energy are reclaimed for you to use as you choose.

Who or what are you willing to forgive in order to make space in your mind and heart?

JOURNAL:

Forgiving God

Sometimes you need to forgive God. Of course, God is not some outside entity that needs forgiveness. It's just that sometimes life hurts so much that it doesn't make sense. At those times, you just need someone to forgive so you can release and move on. Resentment is created by looking back at what could have been when some twist of fate sent your life in another direction, leaving you with wounds and scars. Perhaps it is a loved one departing too soon, a betrayal, or another situation that turned your life upside down that still carries unpleasant energy.

You can wallow in self-pity and be known as the person who survived a horrendous situation. Or, after some processing time, you can decide to face the life that lies before you. You can spoil your future with animosity or let go and forgive your past. To experience joy, you must be free of past pains. Quit comparing the present to how it might have been, and get on with creating how it can be. If you want freedom, get rid of the toxicity. You'll be amazed at how naturally the Good returns.

What situation came up for you as you read today's entry? Try forgiving God for bringing it into your life and see what happens.

JOURNAL:

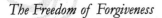

April 25
Still in Prison

There were two prisoners of war who hadn't seen each other for many years since they were freed. When they eventually got together after decades apart, one man asked the other if he had forgiven his captors, to which his friend said, "No way!" The other man replied, "Then you are still in prison." Holding onto the pain of the past, whether physical or emotional, will deny you the freedom and joy your soul yearns to know.

Just because you've forgiven doesn't mean the other person won. It means you are free to live your life. Spirituality calls for you to be more than the personal situation and emotions of your life. Forgiveness may take some time to move through the different levels of the body and mind before freedom is felt again. That is the soul's process for growth. So be patient. Can you be a visionary and see beyond the pull of pain and resentment? You can stay in prison or you can be free, but not both.

Where in your life do you need to be a visionary for your freedom?

JOURNAL:

Casting Call of Consciousness

You don't change a movie by changing the screen. No matter how real the movie seems, the screen only reflects that which is projected onto it. What's going on in your life is only that which you are projecting onto it. As much as you'd like to manipulate the players around you, they are a result of your casting call of consciousness. They and the scenes are just the out-picturing of your beliefs and emotions in form.

The adjustments and retakes cannot be made on the screen nor in the world that lies before you. Rather, you need to go back to what causes the projections to appear. The more proficient you become in dealing with cause and consciousness, the less you will attempt to readjust the material world. The farther you go in the mental realm, the more you'll find it giving way to the spiritual, where God becomes the Executive Producer of your life.

JOURNAL:

April 27

Muggers of Consciousness

Joy is not incidental to your spiritual path—it's vital! Worry, jealousy, anger, self-loathing, revenge, aggression, greed—and the list goes on— are muggers of consciousness. As soon as they arrive, you know there is going to be trouble. Do you pick companionship that is going to mug you or make you sick? Or do you choose what brings you joy and puts a smile on your face?

You don't pick rotting fruit from the produce section of the grocery store. The same holds true for the realm of consciousness. Life is too precious to eat rotten fruit or to be mugged by your thinking. Thought replacement can be challenging, particularly if you've become addicted to the fermented fruit. It will make you sick with a blurred sense of reality. Rotten fruit is not an essential part of your diet, nor are nasty thoughts an integral part of your consciousness. With compassion for yourself, you will make healthier choices. Vital, life-enhancing energy comes from that which brings you joy. Partake of the bountiful fruits of love, joy, peace, freedom, abundance, happiness, compassion— and the list goes on.

What muggers of consciousness are you hanging out with?

JOURNAL:

Trusting in Truth

What is the truth that will set you free? It is the spiritual truth of who you are and how the universal principles of life work. Another way of stating it is: There is a power for good in the universe, and you can use it.

Every situation is transformed, every hurt healed, and each injustice righted when you remember to apply spiritual truths to your life and live from the truth of your being. Often, what you do instead is apply human or worldly wisdom based on cynicism, self-protection, and smallness. This will not set you free, but simply create more of the same mess.

Journal about Truth, the Spiritual Truth needed to set you free in every situation of your life.

JOURNAL:

Heightened Sense

After great surfing, a wonderful workout, or any energetic expression in which the body feels good and the soul comes alive, you have a heightened sense of well-being. In this state of clarity, you feel an excitement about life and increased energy to meet it.

Wouldn't it be nice to have this feeling every day? I'm sure you have lots of reasons for not taking time daily to energize your being.

Take this moment to write down all the ways you could create space in the day to give your body and soul the physical exercise it craves.

JOURNAL:

The Life Force of Food

You body is the temple of God; be aware of what you put into it. A lot of our food today is heavily processed, hormone-fed, chemically toxic, and genetically modified. Does this sound appetizing? Or is it best not to think about it? Do you care that your fruit and vegetables have been sprayed with pesticides that are meant to kill things? Can you actually scrub them enough to get the poison off? More than a chore, it is a lifestyle to become conscientious about the quality of food you put into your body. Genetically modified food doesn't need to be labeled, nor does the type of pesticide used in your food need to be disclosed, even if it does come from the nerve gas family and is suspect of causing cancer and genetic mutations.

You've only been given one body for this lifetime, and life is far more pleasant when your vehicle is running well. What's most important is the consciousness in which your food is ingested. Honoring and activating food's life-giving qualities is as important as gratitude and appreciation for its gifts to your body. Taking the time to pay attention to the taste, textures, and qualities will enhance your dining experience.

How can you be more attentive in your selection process and more present to the experience of what you put into your mouth?

JOURNAL:

May

Free to be Open

May 1-8
The Joy of Children

May 9-13
The Joyous Feminine

May 14-22
Joyous Intuition

May 23-31
The Joy of Listening

Beyond the World of Words

The joy of reading to your child at bedtime is one of those magical gifts from God. It's a memory that lasts a lifetime. The total connection creates a love-experience that can't be explained or forced. It can only be known, felt, and understood beyond the world of words. To be given this experience confirms the potential wonders available to those who choose love.

When you enter the space of love, the search is finished, and you can stop wasting time trying to find people and things to give you this experience. You become free to rest in the realization of love unfolding from within. You let it come to you, not from the outside, but as an outpouring from within the world you have created.

When have you known a love beyond words?

JOURNAL:

Loving All Our Children

All children are new incarnations of Life itself. All children are children of God, and their lives are between them and God. As parents, we have custody of our children for a short time. The biggest challenge parents face is loving their children for who they are and not trying to make them into something they are not. Each child is unique and precious. All children come into the world with their own self-expression and ways of being. The greatest gift we can give our children is to teach them to be themselves.

The job of parents is to socialize children so they grow up confident and capable of negotiating this world. In addition, parents should provide space for children to practice being who they are, allowing them to try on new ways and new identities without fear of ridicule or pressure. Finally, the greatest gift parents can give their children is love, unconditional love for who they are and who they are growing themselves to be.

The job of the community is to provide a safe place for both parent and child, so that there is a safety net of people who love and care for them. This keeps the parents from getting overwhelmed and provides the children with another point of support.

JOURNAL:

Soul Lessons

Putting a sick child to bed leaves one with a helpless, heartbreaking feeling. It's easy to fall back into the old ways of telling God what to do in this situation. "Take away my child's pain and give it to me." Yet, it's important to remember that it's not about healing a sick body, rather seeing the perfect presence of the Divine shining forth. You must get the natural human emotions and concerns out of the way so that you can be a seer of Truth.

It is also a growing, learning time for the child, no matter what his or her chronological age. The soul animating the body has come to learn that consciousness directs form. Children come to know their eternal qualities through this time of fire. They come to realize that they are more than their bodies. As much as you want to protect your children from the discomforts of their world, this world is where they have chosen to take their soul's class. These soul lessons are theirs, not yours. So, stand by, comfort them, love them, and remember to see their true consciousness always coming through. Life is an adventure, even for the small ones.

Where have you been overprotective of someone?

JOURNAL:

Caring for Your Inner Child

Every person carries within themselves an inner child. Your inner child is the one who came to believe certain things about life based on what happened to you as a child. These beliefs are often still at work in your life today. The problem is that, as a child, you saw life through a child's eyes, made decisions with a child's mind, and came to believe things about life from a child's viewpoint. However, now you are an adult. Your inner child no longer has to carry the burden of deciding how life is and what you choose to believe.

Caring for your inner child is called re-parenting. You provide the support, comfort, help, and nurturing to your inner child that you didn't get when you were a child. You remind your inner child that, while he or she may have felt afraid, uncertain, or inadequate, you as the adult can certainly handle things now.

Sit your inner child on your lap and tell him or her that you will take care of everything. Hold your inner child's hand, and explain that you are quite capable of handling life. All your inner chid has to do is play and enjoy the experience.

JOURNAL:

No Stopping the Ripple

Have you ever thrown a stone into a calm lake and watched the ripples come to shore? In life, your actions are the stones you throw. Have you ever stopped to think that there is nothing you can do to stop the ripples from rolling across the calm surface once they have started? Try as you may, you cannot take back the stone once it's been dropped. You have to wait until the energy of the waves dissipates on its own. If you didn't want the response, it would have been better not to have thrown the stone in the first place.

Your actions and words cause ripples of effect in your world. Make sure you are intentional with the energy you release before you make waves, because you cannot stop it once it's been set in motion. The best time to stop the ripples is before you cast the first stone. Be conscious of the impact you are about to make— there's no taking it back.

Where in your life do you regret having a thoughtless action that set in motion a series of events? And where would it be wise to hold back now?

JOURNAL:

Fabricating Evidence

Some people are quick to condemn, pass judgment, criticize, or intentionally tell untruths about others. They use descriptively fabricated evidence in their one-sided storytelling to win people to their perspective. Whatever their reasons or projections may be, you don't have to embrace it— it's their garbage, not yours. If someone offers you the gift of a bag of trash, you are not obligated to accept it. You choose whether or not to accept it. The same is true with peoples' verbal offerings. They are theirs until you accept them. How they are and what they say reveals volumes about their character.

Everyone is a child of God. When you consciously dwell in Spirit, blessings are upon you. Do your best to know, at least on the absolute level, that the very Presence of God can even be found in the place where the betrayal is planned. This awareness is what calls forth the expression of God from the darkest of places. When God is realized, Grace is expressed.

Where in your life do you need to realize the Presence of God more?

JOURNAL:

Knowing the Truth

John 8:32 says, "You shall know the truth and the truth will make you free." Notice that it doesn't say the truth will make you free, but rather *knowing* the truth is what sets you free. Just the fact that God is all there is and that it's all good doesn't assure you a world of fulfillment and joy. To demonstrate this, you must feel the God-realization and bring it to light in everything you do.

It doesn't do any good to run around proclaiming everything is perfect, it's all good, there is no sickness, and the Universe is abundant. Even though these are statements of Spiritual Truth at the absolute level, there may be a human experience contrary to these declarations. Expressing these statements to someone in pain may get you a punch in the nose! When there is pain, compassion from a caring and understanding place is necessary. Each person is on the perfect path at the highest level of his or her awareness in the moment. The life lessons needed for the Soul's growth are coming in their own time and way. It is the God-realization that will be their demonstration. Bringing love to bear in life only assists the process.

Where can you be kinder in your life?

JOURNAL:

Compassion for All

Everyone you meet is a Spiritual Being having a human experience. Regardless of your opinion of others and your desire for them to be different or behave better, they are children of God. Practice seeing this truth about them. Imagine that they, too, are just as worthy of Love as everyone else.

When you do this, it becomes easier to remember that they are also having their own human experience. This means that all the things they do that you don't like are motivated by the same things that motivate you to do what you don't like. Fear, doubt, uncertainty, unworthiness, inadequacy, and a sense of separation are part of your shared human experience. Don't you remember being scared or feeling unworthy, and doing things that you weren't proud of? Realizing this allows your compassion for others to flow from your heart to theirs.

Think about someone who you are having trouble being compassionate toward. Journal about what you think they might be experiencing in their humanness. How does this help you grow your compassion?

JOURNAL:

Celebrating the Feminine

The Divine Feminine possesses the qualities of receptivity, nurturing, and openness. Another way to look at these qualities is from the Chinese notion of *yin* and *yang*. The *yin* qualities, when balanced by the *yang*, are part of what brings you into balance with yourself, and they are available to everyone.

The Divine Feminine reminds us that there is more to life than striving, becoming, achieving, or attaining. While these *yang* qualities are totally worthwhile, there must also be time for listening, receiving, allowing, and growing.

How comfortable are you with your own *yin* qualities? What could you do to invite more of these into your life?

JOURNAL:

Goddess Energy Abounds

Goddess energy profoundly celebrates the beauty, creativity, and joy of all of life. Think of the joy a mother takes in her newborn, seeing her little one as perfect in every way. Think of the beauty in nature, in the verdant fields and lush foliage of the forest and meadows. Think of the amazing creativity behind all of life, growing each tiny seed into a plant that produces beautiful flowers and nourishing fruit.

Goddess energy is present in every girl, woman, and crone you know. Behind the fashion model, the socialite, the wallflower, and the maid lies a deep wellspring of life, even if it seems to be hidden. Look for it, discover its hidden beauty, and call it forth. Watch as it blooms before your very eyes.

Where is the goddess energy present in your life? What can you do to call it forth?

JOURNAL:

Thank You, Mom

Today, journal on the things about your mother for which you are grateful. Whether or not she was there for you, your mother has given you a lot of things in your life. Explore these and see them with gratitude.

JOURNAL:

The Womb of Creativity

There is a place within you where life is stirring to become all that it can be, as you. This inner urge is the very impulse of Life itself, seeking to express more fully as you. This inner creativity is the same urge that causes the seedlings to sprout in the spring and the flowers to burst forth into bloom.

As you feel this inner stirring, nurture it and let it grow. Hold it close to yourself, sharing it only with those you trust to be supportive, for these inner promptings may be fragile and tender for you. Just remember, they come from Life itself, and you are the place where Life is being birthed.

What new idea, new way, new hope, new life is trying to be birthed in you? Are you giving it a safe and sacred space in which to grow?

JOURNAL:

Nurturing Life

Isn't it great to know that every time your water your plants, feed your pets, cloth your child, or plant seeds in your garden, you are nurturing Life? It's just as amazing to realize that every time you praise a colleague, become passionate about an idea, get involved in something that's important to you, or work steadily at what's in front of you, you are nurturing Life just as much.

There are so many ways you can nurture life: in yourself, in those around you, in the natural world, and in the tasks of everyday life. The basis of all nurturing is taking time to care for something. What are you nurturing in your life? Is there something you have neglected to nurture?

JOURNAL:

Pregnant with Possibility

You are pregnant with possibility. You are not stuck within the confines of the life you are experiencing today. There are so many possibilities for your future. How do you know this? Because you live in an infinite Universe. And if it is an infinite Universe, then there are an infinite number of ways that you can express who you are, find joy and happiness, and have a meaningful life!

The Infinite Universe cannot be limited to providing you with only a single opportunity. If you miss one, don't worry! Another one will come along. The Infinite Universe cannot be limited to giving you only two choices—this or that. There is always a third, forth, fifth, or umpteenth possibility. You just haven't seen it yet. That's what it means to live in an unlimited Universe.

You life is pregnant with possibilities. What possibilities are waiting for you that you haven't considered yet? Write down all of them, even if they're foolish or you don't believe you would act upon them. This will open up your creativity to allow the possibilities to come through.

JOURNAL:

Developing Receptivity

Developing receptivity is an exercise in being open, listening to and entertaining the possibilities. First: set aside your agenda, your preconceived ideas about how things are, and your desire or need to have it be a certain way. Second: remember that Spirit is always impelled by Love to express Life more fully. Third: listen for and be open to something that can only be for your highest and best good. And lastly: imagine that there are lots of other possibilities that Spirit knows, even if you don't.

Another spiritual practice that helps develop receptivity is the practice of visioning. Visioning (as opposed to *visualization*) invites you to open yourself to the inflow of Spirit's wisdom and guidance, allowing It to reveal Itself through you.

What is the highest vision Spirit has for your life? Ask yourself this question, then be very still and wait—and listen.

JOURNAL:

Developing Intuition

Everyone has intuition. It's not our intuition that needs to be developed, but rather our ability to listen to it. Most people talk about intuition as the still, small voice that tells you what to do next. However, you may not hear your intuition that way. You may feel it as a nudge or as an inner sense of what to do next. Sometimes intuition comes through the words of others, something someone says or that you read, that suddenly resonates within you. Developing intuition is learning to hear, feel, or sense the way your intuition works and speaks to you.

Begin paying attention to any inner or outer prompting you receive. Watch what happens when you do or do not follow it. Listen for those times when you think to yourself, "I should have...." This will give you clues to when and how your intuition is prompting you.

Journal about your intuition. How does it prompt you? When do you listen and act upon it? When don't you?

JOURNAL:

Your Inner GPS

A Global Positioning System, or GPS, is a helpful piece of electronics that was first used in airplanes and now comes as an option in most cars. When you program where you want to go, it knows where you are and guides you to where you want to be. The directions display on the screen, and some GPS models even tell you when you are off-course and when to turn. You just need to pay attention and follow the directions to your destination.

This is just like your internal navigational system. Spirit knows your present position. You don't need to tell God where you are or what's going on. Spirit knows where you are and has the wisdom to guide you from there to where you want to go—but you have to listen.

It's important to learn how your internal guidance system works—what the pictures on your screen of awareness mean and how to translate them. Everyone comes with a built-in guidance system, but it will do you no good unless you learn how it works. Once you learn how to turn it on and program it, all you need to do is trust what it is telling you and follow the directions.

Where in your life do you need to trust your inner guidance more?

JOURNAL:

Lenses of Projection

Your life as you know it is a projection of your thoughts. You can play the blame game and point your fingers at a dysfunctional family, a betrayal by a friend, a bad economy, or whatever your index of grievances may be for a particular aspect of your life that isn't working. To free yourself and set forth a new projection, ask yourself if there was some way, no matter how small, that you contributed to this experience. That which you don't want to look at in yourself always gets projected onto another.

Your life is a laboratory in which, if you pay attention, you can learn from your creations. It's not about getting it right every time; it's about learning from the feedback of your projections and recasting until you get the world you want to be living in. You give children the space to make mistakes, because they are young and growing. It's important to be gentle with yourself, even though you are older. You are still learning and growing. Age doesn't matter. So tabernacle with the Truth of your being and let Spirit be the lens you focus on your world.

What lens would work best in your projector?

JOURNAL:

Mind is Like a TV

Mind is like a television set with many channels to choose. You get to decide between drama, comedy, horror, or even the history channel. If you don't like what's playing, you can change the channel. You need not get involved with any programming you don't like, because you have the power in your little finger to click the remote.

You need not get focussed on any conditions you see in this world; you've got the power to change your viewing. Become conscious of the God-given dominion to choose what you are going to perceive on the screen of your mind. You don't have to get stuck watching something that makes you cringe just because your partner has decided to watch something you don't like. You still have an infinite amount of viewing options. With all these channels to choose from, do you still complain that there is nothing to watch? Life has given you so many options to choose from that you haven't even begun to discover some of the channels at the far end of the spectrum, but you can click them on at any time.

Are you watching the same story or something new and exciting?

JOURNAL:

Starring You

You are the producer, director, writer, and star of your life story. What kind of drama are you starring in these days? The universe is the executive producer who says "yes" to your direction. It will provide all the resources and people you request through your consciousness. You get to decide whether you are working for a stingy studio on a shoe-string budget or a generous studio who supplies your funding with ease. Your cast of characters includes your choice of over six-billion players. Who is your co-star? Who is your romantic interest? Are they one and the same? Have you given away creative control to your antagonist?

Are the twists and turns to the unfolding plot in your life leading to a happy ending? Are you writing your script from the heart, the head, or just reacting to the run-away drama? If you were to review and add some re-writes, what new scenes and actors would you add to your life story?

JOURNAL:

Which Way to Go?

Are you stuck wondering what the "right" choice is? Does this keep you paralyzed and stuck, unable to make a decision or move forward? Ask yourself, "What's the worst that can happen?" Usually, the answer is, "It won't work out" or "I'll have made a mistake."

The beauty of living from spiritual principles is that you can make a new choice at any moment. A mistake is only a mistake if you don't learn from it.

Journal about what choice you need to make to move you forward? What's the worst that can happen?

JOURNAL:

A Lift in Perspective

As you gain altitude in flight, going higher and higher, your vision expands and you see a lot more below than when you were sitting on the ground. The landscape expands before your eyes, revealing streams, trees, valleys, and mountains that you couldn't see before you took off. It's not that they were added to the Earth as your view elevated; they were there the whole time, waiting to be seen. They were already there; the shift took place in *you.*

The same is true of the spiritual kingdom— it has already been given. Spirit hasn't held anything back for later. It is all available to you when you rise in consciousness and expand the view. You free your soul's limitations by knowing that everything you need in life is already available and awaiting your recognition.

Where in your life could you use a lift in perspective?

JOURNAL:

How Much Is Enough?

The outside world cannot be any better than your state of consciousness. If there is something not working in your experience, then there is something that needs to be known by you. If there is nothing in you that will respond to the negativity of the world, the troubles of the world cannot find a home in your life and will pass you by.

Life keeps talking to you, giving you feedback as to where your thinking is. But are you attentive? If not, the voice will get louder and louder. How much pain do you want before you are sure you want no more? The Universe loves you so much that it was set up to return to you specific information about where you are on your journey. You get to decide. Do you want to keep going in the direction in which you're headed, or do you want to change course? It's totally your choice, if you've been paying attention.

Where haven't you been listening? Where have you had enough?

JOURNAL:

Deep Listening

Listening to the profound silence of nature, I realize there is much to be heard. In this deep hearing exists a feeling, an understanding of the connectedness of all life, and a sense of well-being. What would it be like to transfer this kind of listening to your friends, so that you could actually feel what they were saying? What if you listened so deeply that no matter what they had to say, they would feel secure and welcome in your presence? They would feel your love so much that they'd know they were safe to say anything, and they would be heard and understood.

You can listen like this any time you care enough to turn off your head chatter. Just dial into that which is presenting itself to your awareness. Tune out anything else you bring to the moment. Trust what is coming, and you'll know what to say, do, or be.

Try it with someone you love today. What can you hear beyond the words being spoken?

JOURNAL:

May 25
"Ceda!"

When driving across small, one-lane bridges in the United States, the driver who arrives first has the right of way over the driver who got there second. It seems logical and simple. Since single-lane bridges are a common part of the driving experience in Costa Rica, I practiced the same courtesy there. Yet, even when I was the first to arrive at the bridge and started crossing, I sometimes received strange looks and shouts of, "Ceda! Ceda! Ceda!" Only later did I come to learn that every bridge has a sign on one side that says "Ceda." I now know "ceda" means "Yield." It doesn't matter who gets to the bridge first; it's the person who is on the "ceda" side who is supposed to yield.

In life, we sometimes push ahead because we think we have the right of way, even when it's really our turn to yield and let the traffic of our life pass us by so the way is made clear. Instead of being first to cross, try yielding to Spirit and allow the path to open up before you.

Where in your life would it be helpful to yield and have Spirit go before you?

JOURNAL:

A Higher Understanding

The capacity to enter the Divine Realization is always available. No matter where you find yourself standing in life, you can always turn and face God. In this turning, the self that has been hurt diminishes and gives way to the emergence of the Higher Understanding. You are then freed from the thoughts of human thinking and begin to experience the higher perception of that which truly is.

There is far more clarity looking out from the peak above the clouds of confusion than looking up through the fog of the lowlands. Higher states of awareness are available to and for everyone at all times. This knowing dissipates any of the dense perceptions that hold you back.

What thoughts are weighing you down that you'd like to give up?

JOURNAL:

What Tunes are You Playing?

What tune is playing on your cosmic iPod? What sound bytes are pumping into your head? When you go to the ocean, do you hear the theme from "Jaws" or Jimmy Buffet's "Margaritaville"? The tune you listen to will conjure up feelings, but which ones make you happy and smile? Have you ever thought about playing the theme from "Rocky" as you put a deal together?

Any phrase you repeat moves you up or down the energetic scale. It's about how you shift the transmission of consciousness. What you say to yourself makes all the difference as to how you experience life. The tunes you play and the words you say to yourself determine how you see life.

JOURNAL:

Delayed for a Reason

When a plane gets delayed, there's not much you can do about it. I'm always amazed at individuals who go berserk on the airline employee at the check-in counter, as if it's that person's fault. If there is something wrong with the plane, you don't want to discover it when you're at thirty thousand feet. If the aircraft isn't at the gate, you are not going to make it show up any quicker by expressing your fury.

Emotional outbursts do not attract spiritual realization. Neither does falling too easily into victim consciousness. You have within you the capacity to rise above any situation in life. Spiritual perspectives, with their myriad of possible insights, fill your awareness when they are invited, no matter what the conditions may be.

If you prefer peace, patience, and understanding, then you must stop filling your mind with their opposites.

Where are you not allowing space in your thoughts for peace?

JOURNAL:

Surprises of Enchantment

Planning a day or having a goal are good ways to make sure your precious energy is not lost or wasted. Having an idea about where you are headed is always helpful. Yet, you still want to be flexible enough to be able to embrace the unexpected gifts along the path. Spirit will continue to offer surprises of enchantment, but do you make space for them?

When life throws unexpected changes at you, are you able to trust yourself enough to improvise and go with the flow? When you are connected with the Source, instead of your fears, control gives way to the gifts of spontaneous co-creation for greater Good. Can you make plans and still remain unattached enough to change as life offers you new perspectives on the path? You can't even begin to see all the Good coming your direction. Get out and get going, so the Greater Good can happen to you!

Where in your life could you use more flexibility?

JOURNAL:

Filthy Filters of Awareness

Have you ever looked at someone wearing filthy glasses and wondered how he could see through those things? Somehow, he grew accustomed to seeing through the messy filters and no longer perceives any difference. This didn't happen from some big splash in a puddle or as a result of an instant dandruff dump. If this were the case, he would have noticed and cleaned the glasses right away. It probably accumulated little by little throughout the course of the day. Only a stranger passing by would notice the drastic difference between clear and not clear.

It's the gradually accumulating annoyances that add up without conscious awareness that weigh you down. You know when you have to deal with the big things in life; it's all the un-addressed, little issues that will cloud the beauty of your world. Just as one regularly takes off his or her glasses to clean them, you, too, need to stop throughout the course of the day, consistently checking in to see what needs to be cleaned up and thrown out. Otherwise, you'll be looking through filthy filters of awareness.

Is there a place in your life where you don't see any good choices?

JOURNAL:

Trackless Steps

Catch Spirit by relaxing into It. The more you chase It, the more illusive It becomes. Listen and wait upon the Lord, and something will come through. It's not necessarily a message or some kind of earthshaking, transformative insight; it might just be a feeling of pressure releasing, a burden dissolving, or just a greater sense of peace. This kind of high feeling is what can carry you through a day or a challenge.

As you move through life, you don't want to leave a wake of hurt that will have to be dealt with at a later time. Let every step you take be trackless, so that nothing can come back to haunt you. The more time you spend resting in the higher realm, the greater the opportunity for Spirit's spontaneous gifts of Grace to be revealed on your path. Stop chasing after that peaceful place. Keep you mind stayed on the Divine, and you will find all Good added unto you.

JOURNAL:

Free to be Strong

Inner Strength

You are the very presence of Spirit, Life Itself, as you. Whatever you may be facing in your life, you have all the strength and courage to deal with it, because you have the entire strength of the Universe at your back.

Think about the power and strength that it takes to create a universe, to keep all the planets spinning in their orbits, to keep evolution unfolding and life moving forward. That is the strength you can rely on. Surely it's big enough and strong enough for what you are facing.

Inner strength comes from the realization that you are not alone—that you are not the source of your life, and that you don't have to be. Inner strength is the realization that all the strength you will ever need is right where you are.

JOURNAL:

You're in Charge

You are in charge of your life, whether you like it or not. Even when you don't feel like you're in charge, you are. Often, we don't feel like we're in charge of our lives because someone or something is behaving in a way that we don't like. We want them to stop or change. What we try to do, then, is control the situation or the person. And, of course, this is not something we have control over, so we end up feeling like we're not in charge of our own lives at all.

While you don't have control over anything outside of yourself, you do have control over the one thing that will absolutely cause you to be in charge of your life—your mind. You are in control of the thoughts you think, the attitudes you assume, and your perspective on things.

Where in your life do you need to let go of control? Where in your mind do you need to start being in charge?

JOURNAL:

The Purpose of Life

Everyone wants to know what the purpose of life is. What we also want to know is, what is the purpose of *my* life? Do you know the purpose of your life?

The way to see the purpose of life is to realize that Life is forever seeking to express Itself, be Itself, and become Itself through all of creation. And this includes *you!* Life's purpose for you is to experience and express what life is like *as* you!

So what is life, *as you?* What do you want to express and experience that is uniquely yours? What are your precious and idiosyncratic ways of being and looking at life that make you feel the most complete, the most satisfied, and the most giving? Write about these ideas today.

JOURNAL:

Setting Your Course

You are free to choose your course in life. You choose the direction, then set the sails of your life to work with whatever winds blow. The biggest question to ask when setting your course is, "Where do you want to go?"

Where do you want to end up next week, next year, next decade? When you don't think about these things, you react to life's winds without purpose or direction. If you don't decide where you want to go, you'll most likely end up someplace else.

Certainly, there are times to simply drive off in whatever direction suits your fancy. This can be a wonderful adventure, full of serendipitous and wondrous experiences. And you are free to choose this.

However, if you are concerned about where you may end up, or if you actually want to choose where you end up, then you have to set your course.

Where are you going?

JOURNAL:

Power vs. Force

You may have come to believe that having power over things or people is the only way you'll get what you need. You may have come to believe that you have no power and are a victim of life. You may have come to believe that power is a dirty word, so you distance yourself from exercising the power that you have.

Yet, there is a powerful place in life that invites us to stand up for what we believe, ask for what we want, and offer our gift without restriction or shame. This place is our place of personal power.

Often, this power is confused with a desire or attitude of force—seeking to force something to happen, force someone to understand or change, or force yourself to accept or accommodate.

Force is a relentless energy, trying to make something happen. Power is a grounded energy, from which we shall not be moved.

Where are you trying to apply force? Where are you avoiding your power?

JOURNAL:

Whose Will?

Where in your life have you forced your will upon a situation? A lot of trouble comes when you misuse your willpower. When do you attack a problem with force, rather than listen for the highest answer to present itself, allowing it to unfold in its perfect time? When a situation is not unfolding effortlessly, it's a call to go to God.

Have you ever forced your will with a jigsaw puzzle piece, attempting to make it fit into the wrong place in a puzzle? It's not a pretty picture, but provides instant feedback that it's not right. Your world may not always give you instant feedback, but you will get delayed fallout. When you go to a higher wisdom and call it forth into a particular situation, let go of your will and allow God's will and wisdom to prevail. Spirit can only do for you what you will allow It to do through you.

Where in your life do you need to get out of the way so that Spirit can show up?

JOURNAL:

Cultivating Willingness

Life offers a wonderful paradox between choosing your direction and being willing to be shown what's next. Your job is to pick a direction and an end result, like getting a new job or having a more meaningful life. Once you've chosen the direction, cultivate the willingness to act on whatever task seems like the next thing to do. This allows you to be open and flexible as opportunities and possibilities present themselves. As you become willing to try different ideas or explore various forks in the road, you will find that more possibilities present themselves.

Cultivating willingness also helps you get unstuck in any area of your life. Willingness to try something new, make a change, or simply ask for help is the first step of forward motion. Being stuck is often simply an unwillingness to face the fact that something needs to change or be done differently. This is easier to face when you have cultivated willingness.

Where do you need to cultivate willingness in your life?

JOURNAL:

The Power of Will

Moving forward in your life, in the direction of your choosing, requires that you stay committed and dedicated to your goal. This is the act of a disciplined will.

Now, this is not willpower. You are not willing something to happen or trying to make it happen with your own personal force. This just makes people tired and stressed.

The correct use of will is using it to focus on the end result, being aware of opportunities as they present themselves, while staying disciplined to the course you have set for yourself. You can think of the power of your will as the focusing of a camera lens. You determine what you will focus on, but the camera actually takes the picture.

Are you exhausting yourself by trying to make things happen? Are you depressing yourself by constantly changing your mind or getting off course? Or, are you staying focused on your goal while being flexible about the process?

JOURNAL:

Exhilarating

Why do some people watch horror movies or go bungee jumping? There is some kind of exhilaration those choices bring to the soul. Believing we have many lifetimes and this is only one stopping place on our evolving journey, one frame of the film of a long movie, the exhilaration that comes from certain life events, choices or living environments is like the experience of choosing to watch a horror flick. It, too, shall pass, like the end of the movie. Sometimes completing this go-round in this world plane is like walking out at the end of the show.

Where you find yourself is no mistake. You contributed to getting yourself into that life situation, including where you were born. You are an unfolding state of consciousness, in which your outer world of form will never be any greater than your inner awareness. Just as one can know all is fine while plummeting through the air or being scared out of their seats, so, too, the degree to which you become consciously aware of the Presence of God in the apparent opposite can also be exhilarating.

What exhilarating experience are you done with in your life?

JOURNAL:

The *What*, not the *How*

There is a Universal power and principle—the Law of Cause and Effect—that always operates in your life. It constantly takes your desires, goals, attitudes, and beliefs as the mold for your life, and creates your reality out of that mold.

You don't have to ask this Law to operate, and you don't have to make it work. All you have to do is pay attention to the mold you are creating. You can change your desires, goals, attitudes, and beliefs by using conscious and constructive intentionality and thinking. This will change your mold. You can then trust the Law to change your life.

Trusting the Law means that you don't meddle with *how* these change will come about. You stay focused on the mold. The Law will take care of the rest.

Is there anywhere in your life that you are trying to control the *how* and not trusting the Law?

JOURNAL:

Steep Slippery Steps

I didn't get to the mountain monasteries of Tibet in a day. It was a long journey that began with preparations, tens of thousands of steps up steep and often slippery slopes with the angelic help of Sherpas, and many a below-freezing night in a pup tent. Every step at extreme altitudes was slow and laborious.

Yet, it was essential that I put one boot in front of the other to achieve my vision. None of us get there instantly. It's about enjoying the views, the camaraderie, the journey, learning more about your body and mind, and embracing the people and villages along the way. Every step presents a lesson that you'd never get sitting in the cold assembly halls of a monastery. Your spiritual achievement doesn't come from reading, but from getting out of your safe and comfortable chair to create events leading to your destination. So, embark on the steep, slippery climb. Look out upon the vistas. You'll come to know you are already in Shangri-la.

Where do you need to get out and get going?

JOURNAL:

Never Give Up

Not yet getting what you prayed for simply means that the answer to your prayer hasn't arrived. Not yet achieving your goal simply means that there is more to come, more to learn, and more to accomplish.

As long as you stay true to the end result, God will make it happen. Sometimes, it seems like the very atoms and molecules of the Universe Itself need to be rearranged in order for you to achieve your heart's desire. This may take some time.

In the meanwhile, stay focused on your goal. Stay committed to your path. Don't give up, and Life won't give up on you. You are free, of course, to change your mind and choose something else. But make sure it's a choice, not simply giving up.

JOURNAL:

Beyond Imagination

The ability to concentrate allows you to bring vitality and clarity to whatever you are doing, whether you are writing, engaging in a sport, or plotting a heist. This power of concentration enhances your suffering or your well-being. It gives you access to deeper states of awareness. Your heightened awareness moves in the direction of your focus. Imagine if you pointed this focus toward happiness or love, spending an extended amount of time concentrating and going deep within. The new realms of possibilities that will open to you are beyond your present imagination.

Whole new realms await your journeying. The more time you give to the practice of concentration, the more the mind's wanderings subside, and the side trips your mind takes diminish. You are freed from tension and distraction. You move beyond the ordinary sensing to an extraordinary understanding.

Where in your life do you need to take more time to focus?

JOURNAL:

Living in a Parallel Universe

Once, I got a mosquito bite in the Grand Canyon. Suddenly, the entire trip became about the mosquito bite. It didn't matter that the grandest of America's canyons spread out before me. A pesky bite drew my attention away from this enormous expression of God's beauty. I *became* a mosquito bite—cut off from the larger reality.

The power of your mind is strong and can take you on a detour from your God experience. It can set you up in a parallel universe, fixated on infinitesimal nothingness. You must remember who you are: an heir to the kingdom of God that lies before you. You do this by feeling your connection with the Source, and not to any outside source. Stop identifying with the small things, the distractions of pains, mistakes, and victimizations that don't serve you—you are not these things. You cannot serve two masters. As Joshua said, "As for me and my house, we will serve the Lord."

Where in your life are you being distracted?

JOURNAL:

June 15
Living in Commitment

Your commitment is your decision about who you are going to be and how you are going to live. Your commitments that which you value, those things that are important and meaningful to you. Every time you make a choice, you demonstrate your commitments. These choices are available every day.

If someone were to look at your life, to what would they say you have been committed? Is this how you want your life to speak?

JOURNAL:

Staying Focused

One of the most powerful spiritual tools available is your ability to stay focused on your goal, regardless of the twists and turns in the road. Keeping yourself fixed on the end result allows you to negotiate the path—with all its many hills and valleys—without getting bored, frustrated, or discouraged. These feelings arise when you mistake a particular moment or event along the path as the end result, or you think the obstacles are too big for you to overcome.

With God, all things are possible. Any obstacle can be overcome and every challenge met through sustained effort and focus. What obstacle or challenge is presenting itself to you? What do you need to stay focused on instead?

JOURNAL:

June 17
What Do You Want?

Today, journal about what you want in life. Not what you think you should want or what you were told to want. But what you actually want.

Ask yourself over and over and over: "What do I want?" Then, see what unfolds!

JOURNAL:

Sustainable Energy

Attempting to keep the world going with unsustainable resources is like trying to carry water in a strainer—it doesn't work. The water will pour out quickly. But if you use sustainable energy, such as wind or light, the infinite supply is inexhaustible with undiminished expression everywhere. When running your life on your own energy supply, i.e., forcing things to happen with your mental directions, you have only so much earthly energy to sustain the motion.

Become more aware of the inexhaustible life force that surrounds you. This life energy permeates all space; it is the intelligence which guides the universe, looking to move through your avenue of expression. It is everywhere available. So, move away from using yourself, and move toward being the channel through which Spirit pours forth into distinctive earthly activities.

Where would you like to experience more of the life force?

JOURNAL:

June 19
The Gaia Principle

Shamans have been telling us for thousands of years that the Earth is a vibrant, living entity. Recently, scientists and environmentalists have come to the same conclusion. Our Earth is a single organism, living and breathing and growing as One. Anther way to think of this is that the Earth is a huge ecosystem in which every part is dependant upon every other part. This is called the Gaia Principle.

Astronauts have come home from space with beautiful images and profound experiences of realizing this Oneness. Having seen this truth, they have reminded us that our divisions are arbitrary and that what happens at one place on Earth affects the whole.

Gaia has created a part of Itself that can detach and reflect upon the whole. This part is the human species. Thus, Gaia gets to see and contemplate Itself through us.

JOURNAL:

Honoring the Great Spirit

Father Sky above balances Great Mother Earth below. You stand on Mother Earth and, like the trees, stretch up toward the Great Spirit. This is the very presence of Life that creates all things and pulls you forward toward the greater yet-to-be.

Creation is ever unfolding, and you are a part of the expansion. Your very life is a gift from the Great Spirit. So, what are you doing with it? You honor the Great Spirit to the extent that you make something of yourself and your life.

What are you making of your life? What are you creating with it?

JOURNAL:

Befriending the Masculine

Sometimes, it can be challenging to know what to do in life or to feel confident in moving ahead. Sometimes direct action is called for, but you feel hesitation or tentativeness. Hanging back or doing nothing can cause as much stress as doing too much.

You have access to a powerful, directive, forward moving energy. This is the masculine, creator, *yang* energy within you. *Yang* balances the *yin* energy of receptivity, allowing, and openness. Both are required for a mature, healthy, joyous life.

Where are you hanging back in your life, not willing to move forward? Where could you be more direct, assertive, or powerful? What would it take for you to bring that part of you fully into your life?

JOURNAL:

God, the Father

Jesus radically altered our relationship with the Creator when he referred to the Creator as *Abba* or *Father*. While this does not mean that God comes to us in the image of a man or a parent (especially an abusive or absent one), it does make it possible for us to be related to God as a part of God's family.

Imagine the most perfect father, one who supports his family, teaches his children, and invites them into the family business. What is God's family business? Creation, itself! And *you* are invited to be a part of it. You are the heir to God's kingdom—all of creation. And your Father has given you all the tools you need to co-create with Him.

What are you doing with the family business in your life?

JOURNAL:

June 23
Thank You, Dad

Being a dad is one of the hardest jobs in the world. While not every dad is perfect, each one was doing the best he could with what he knew.

What are you grateful for that your dad taught you? What activities did you do with him that you are grateful for? What do you need to forgive your dad for? Can you see that he was doing the best he could?

JOURNAL:

God's Grip

Do you remember how secure you felt as a child when you held your dad's hand? Bring on the lions, tigers, and bears, because you knew you were safe with your dad. As you walk through the jungles of your life, it's nice to know Dad's hand is still there. Is God this familiar to you?

The omnipresent aspect of the Father/Mother God allows you to know that you walk with Spirit. When health challenges rustle around your body, financial issues fill the headlines, or relationships appear scary, remember that you are safe in God's hands no matter what. You don't need to pray to overcome any of these earthly situations, because you are holding God's hand. All you ever need to hold onto is the realization that the Presence is always with you.

Where in you life would you like to feel God's reassuring grip?

JOURNAL:

Mind Gymnastics

It's hard to be anxious and trust God at the same time. You can choose to live with stress and allow something on the outside to control how you feel on the inside, or you can deal with what's at hand and not add any extra personal emotions to it. The Omnipotent is far greater than anything going on in your world. There will always be logical reasons to not change your ways. You'll always be challenged to slip back into previous patterns of behavior. It may not be easy to let go of your familiar friend called *worry*.

The way to stop worrying is to *just stop it*. Quit feeding it. Push past the initial awkwardness of modification. Once you move beyond the ache of starving the stress away, you'll establish a comfortable, new way of being. It's important to not only stop the mental gymnastics that are bringing you down, but to add some faith-filled affirmative thoughts to fill the void. Try peace, calm, and trust, rather than the internal racing.

JOURNAL:

Confused

When people say they're confused, they're really just not dealing with what's going on. They tend to have an underlining energy that doesn't want to be owned. I like to ask these people, "If you weren't confused, what would you be feeling or doing?" It's interesting how often that question cuts through the confusion and releases a strong perspective.

There is something inside you that always knows what you want and is not confused. So, stop giving your power away to the fear of making an incorrect expression. Instead of caring about appearances and perception, take a stand for what your soul knows. The demonstration of your good grows out of your ability to know. Be bold and don't hold back. You know.!

What issues or lack of expression are you no longer willing to be confused about? If you weren't confused, what would you be feeling or doing?

JOURNAL:

Feeling your Feelings

Emotions are responses to thoughts and beliefs that are triggered when something happens. Usually, those thoughts and beliefs are so buried in our past that we don't even realize that we are reacting to them. Perhaps the best response to our feelings is to allow ourselves to feel them, express them appropriately, and know that they are not the truth of our situation.

Practice allowing yourself to feel your feelings without identifying yourself with those feelings. Rather than "I am mad," how about "I feel mad." When you experience a feeling, let yourself feel it, then allow it to move up and out. This way it doesn't get stuck and become an illness or emotional burden.

What feelings are being triggered in your life these days?

JOURNAL:

The Same Starting Place

Sailing can inspire you. You catch an invisible force—the wind—and off you go. Your destination may be straight ahead, but if the winds are not going in that direction, you must "tack" from one side to the other, moving you incrementally closer to your goal. Though many sailors leave from the same harbor with the same wind, each will choose journeys and destinations that will be different from anyone else's.

We each come into this world from the same realm, armed with infinite possible journeys, destinations, and adventures, all awaiting our choice. We all catch the same divine winds. We can navigate on course or off, ever moving ourselves closer to our intentions. If we stop paying attention, the winds will push us in whatever direction they are blowing. It may not be where you want to go, so navigate wisely.

Are there any cross-winds blowing you in a direction don't want to go?

JOURNAL:

Feeling like a Runaway Train

I saw the wreckage of several lumber-filled train cars strewn across the ground. The train had derailed while going around a curve on a hill. I was later informed that a wedge under the wheels of these cars had become dislodged while they were awaiting their coupling. A tiny wedge under a front wheel was the only thing holding back these massive cars from going downhill on their own. When the wedge failed, the cars rolled down the track with too much speed to handle the curve.

In life, you can sometimes let up on the brakes before you're ready to head down the track. When there is no engineer to control the power and momentum, there will be a wreck. It is essential in life to be appropriately equipped when rolling out of the station. When you remember to be coupled with the greatest engineer of them all, you won't have a runaway.

Is there a place in your life where you feel like a runaway train?

JOURNAL:

Tune Out or Deal with it

When you decide to tune out rather than deal with it—whatever "it" is—you don't get to be selective. The life force moves away when you disconnect, leaving only enough for basic sustenance. Tuning out leaves you apathetic and numb instead of joyous and excited. At first it might feel good not having to deal with the issue at hand, but you actually feel nothing when you're turned off. You become more emotionally and energetically removed from life. Then it gets harder to turn on the switch to re-enter your world.

When you hit the "off" button, you deny yourself all your heart's desires. You can't be turned off and turned on at the same time. When you are turned off, you are a turn-off to be around. A passionless life is not an inviting environment for friendship, intimacy, and honesty.

What in your life have you been hoping would go away without your having to deal with it?

JOURNAL:

Free to Create Your Life

July 1-8
Joyous Freedom

July 9-16
Joy of Creativity

July 17-24
Joy of Using Your Imagination

July 25-31
Joy of Seeing Reality

Celebrating Your Dance

You dance through life to your own particular beat, writing your own music and creating your own steps.

What dance are you dancing? Celebrate it! Is there a new dance you want to learn? Go for it! Get out on the dance floor of life and shake your booty!

JOURNAL:

Tune Within

Have you ever caught a glimpse of something at the edge of your vision, a quick flash of an image moving right beyond your conscious awareness, just beyond your grasp? You see something there, but it remains elusive.

Life has more for you than you can see. Your frustration to get it actually pushes it away, making it harder to catch. The frustration exists in your dream life, not in your true life. Separation exists in the belief that something exists outside Spirit and not in the Omnipresent. You break the bonds of limitation when you stop looking out and turn within to see what wants to be known in your field of awareness.

What's been dancing around your periphery?

JOURNAL:

Dream Big & Bold

What is your deepest longing? What is your boldest dream? What is your biggest, most outrageous desire?

What if you fail? What if you never try? If you were on your death bed, what would you want to say about your life? What do you want to leave as your legacy?

Explore your biggest and boldest dreams. What is holding you back? How could you move forward?

JOURNAL:

Freedom

This day is a reminder of your freedom. People have given so much over generations so that you could make choices today based upon your heart's desires, rather than from a reactionary fear. The Declaration of Independence says, "All are created equal and endowed by the creator with inalienable rights. Among these are life, liberty, and the pursuit of happiness." Does your life reflect these rights? Benjamin Franklin said, "Freedom is not a gift bestowed on us by other men, but a right that belongs to us by the laws of God and nature."

Have you been abdicating your freedom by not living in a way that brings you joy and happiness? The laws of nature conspire to support your freedom. Do you pursue that which brings you happiness, or give in to the downward pull of fear? Many are still under the belief they have to give their lives over to the dictates of others'. Yet even today, people are still giving their lives for you to be free. Are you making their sacrifice worth it?

Where in your world could you reclaim more freedom?

JOURNAL:

The Freedom to Create

Your life is like a garden. You are free to plant in it whatever you choose. You can plant an herb garden to help flavor your food. You can plant a vegetable garden to support your family. You can plant a flower garden to beautify your home. You can plant a wild flower or cottage garden for a riot of color outside. You can plant a forest for fuel or as shelter for wildlife. Or you can plant any combination you'd like. You are free to create your life in the same way.

Explore what you've been planting in the garden of your life. Does it suit and satisfy you? Explore what you would like to create differently. Remember that you are free to do so.

JOURNAL:

Freedom to Be Who You Are

There is only one Divine Plan for you: the Divine Plan of Freedom. To think that you have been given free will, choice, and creativity without the opportunity to use them would be to imagine a cruel and unloving God who requires you to conform to a predetermined path and viewpoint.

God's gift is the impulsion of Life to Be You! You are free to express that in whatever way seems most true to who you are and how you want your life to be.

Journal about having the freedom to be who you are. What are you doing with it?

JOURNAL:

You Won't Return the Same

Without a conscious connection to your Higher Self, you wander like a lost child with a sense that something's missing, something vital and comforting. Siddhartha and King Arthur searched for it, indigenous people go on vision quests for it, and much folklore involves going on this quest and leaving the familiar behind. What is this indescribable yearning for this unknown something? What is it that is calling you to go beyond what you know?

The call to connect spiritually is one of the strongest and most empowering forces in your life. The inner pull for awakening will transform everything you know. This desire may have laid dormant for years, but when life shifts and the desire raises its head, watch out! You will become alive like you never have before. But be careful: if you choose to follow this call, you won't come back the same.

JOURNAL:

God Sightings

You have to pay attention when doing your spiritual work; you just might end up running into God everywhere you turn. You'll be surprised how you keep bumping into It everywhere. Not only will you see Spirit looking back at you from the eyes of children, but grumpy people will become nice at checkout stands. You'll find understanding voices at customer service, challenging situations will gracefully resolve, and the list goes on.

When you move past the "gimme, gimme" type of prayer and bask in the glow of the Presence just for the sake of being in the Divine Vibe, then God sightings start happening all around you. You have tuned into the essence of what *is*, rather than what's missing. When you are at the point where you have nothing you want, but continue to be in the Presence of God, you will see Spirit everywhere.

When were there times you were surprised by the sudden appearance of the Divine?

JOURNAL:

The Impulsion to Create

You were born with an innate impulsion to express and create the life that is uniquely yours. This impulsion is the very heartbeat of Life itself, as it seeks to express as you, through your life.

Now, creating doesn't mean only art or music, although it certainly may. You are designed to create your life with your thoughts, attitudes, desires, and gifts. Together, these are your tools, and your life is your canvas. You are free to create beauty, meaning, or self-expression in whatever way calls to you - through your work, your family, your hobbies, your giving, and your volunteering. You are also free to create the life you choose through your beliefs, your expectations, your willingness to grow, and your spiritual connection.

What are you creating in your life today?

JOURNAL:

The Creativity of Spirit

Look around at the amazing variety of life—a starfish, a bumble bee, an eagle, an oak tree, a galaxy, a quark, an atom. Each expresses life so differently. Think about the creativity of Spirit to become this vast array of life and the creativity necessary to sustain all the different kinds of creation. That is the infinite Creativity of Spirit.

Since this same life is your life right now, this creativity is available to you. The incredible dance of creation is happening right where you are, every day.

Feel the dance of creativity through you. Journal on the ways you are creative in your life—from the arts to ideas, from cooking to raising your children, or organizing your work.

JOURNAL:

Finding Your Creativity

Do you remember attending art classes as a kid? Did you enjoy the feel of the clay and the smell of the paints? Or did you dread the inevitable comparison and correction by the teacher? Somewhere along the line, did you decide you just weren't creative?

The truth is, you create something in your life everyday. You create a home; you create a room; you create a family or friendships; you create a party, a gathering, a retreat, or a vacation; you create ideas and plans; you create possibilities and dreams. You are always creating.

With what materials—ideas, people, objects, sounds, smells, colors, tastes—do you like to create? What do you like to create? Explore your own creativity.

JOURNAL:

Co-Creating with God

The Law of Cause and Effect is the orderly process through which the impulsion of Spirit becomes manifest creation. When Spirit said, "Let there be Light," there was light—not a tomato. This Law works from the idea to the effect, constantly manifesting creation.

You, having been made in the image and likeness of God, are a microcosm of the macrocosm. The Law of Cause and Effect works in your life all the time. You can count on this, trust it, and use it for good in your life and in the world. Both you and God use the Law of Cause and Effect: you co-create your life with Spirit, while God busily creates Life.

What causes and ideas are you setting into motion through your thoughts, attitudes, beliefs, and feelings? Do you rely on the Power of God, the constant Law of Creation, to co-create your life? Or are you trying to do it all on your own?

JOURNAL:

Joyously Creative

Life is like Play-Doh—there are lots of colors to choose from. You can mash it around to make it soft and pliable. Then, you get to shape it into whatever suits your fancy.

Explore what it would be like to live your life this way. Journal about the things you'd make. Let yourself play!

JOURNAL:

Life is Creative

All of creation is bursting with life. This Life is the One Life that is the creative Power and Presence behind and within everything. It is the impulse to become, to grow, to expand, and, then, to express.

You can see this in the vigor of the seedling as it pushes up through the earth. You can see it in the vast, painted fields of flowers in their wild array of beauty. You can feel it in the burgeoning, growing season as the fruit ripens.

Where is life bursting forth through you? What is trying to become and grow, express and expand in you life?

JOURNAL:

Playing with your Medium

Artists create in various mediums—paint, clay, wood, light, movement, sound, and the list goes on. You are the artist, and your medium is your life, which includes your thoughts, feelings, attitudes, beliefs, loves, and expectations, as well as the results, people, places, events, and circumstances.

What is your primary medium? Are you using your thoughts or the circumstances around you? Explore the medium of your life. Journal about other mediums you could be using to create your life and those you'd like to stop using. Imagine yourself playing with your life as if it were your artistic medium. What would change?

JOURNAL:

I am Creative

How many times have you said, "I am not creative," when you actually meant that you don't draw, paint, write, or sing? Now is the time to really explore this message. Do you equate creativity with artistic talent? Did someone teach you this or did you decide it for yourself?

One of the fundamental characteristics of Life is that it is always creating. You are constantly co-creating your life with Spirit and Universal Law. How can you co-create when you believe you are not creative?

Creativity, as you have explored, comes in many forms and fashions: ideas, solutions, homes, child rearing, relationships, possibilities, product or sales approaches, or techniques for staying focused on the job.

List ten ways that have nothing to do with arts and crafts in which you are creative. Then, start reminding yourself just how creative you really are!

JOURNAL:

Where Head Meets Heart

The dreams in your head and the longings of your heart meet in the creative sea of your imagination. Your head creates plans and ideas, but it can become obsessed with worrying and trying to figure out everthing. Your heart knows what you desire and what your gifts are, but it can become obsessed with fear and false feelings.

Your head and heart meet in the safety of your imagination. Here, you can play out your dreams and plans and delve into their truths and their unfolding processes. It is also in your imagination where you feel your feelings and play out the decisions you might make based on those feelings, seeing if they lead you into expansion and greater self-expression.

Your imagination is the fertile sea of creativity in which you can explore who you are and who you want to become. Try it today.

JOURNAL:

Imagining Your Life

Science of Mind founder Ernest Holmes taught that you don't get what you want; you get who you are. This means that for you to experience a different life, you must become the person who has that life. How do you do that? You imagine it.

Imagine yourself in healthy relationships. Imagine yourself having meaningful and fulfilling work. Imagine yourself joyfully experiencing life. Your brain doesn't know the difference between a real or imagined experience. Thus, the more completely you imagine yourself to be the person having that experience, the more completely the mold is created.

Journal about this reality. Become it in your imagination and journal about its unfolding.

JOURNAL:

Living in the Conversation

It is easy to start thinking you live in the situations of the world, when you are actually living in the *conversations* of the world. When your monologue is about fear, struggle, and loss, that's where you get to dwell. If your conversations are about thanksgiving, joy, and creation, then you will live there. Your inner and outer chatter focuses your energy and creates your walk through life.

You are the commentator of your world. But, unlike analysts who report the facts after they happen, you forecast things to come. You call it before it happens. So, pay attention to your self-fulfilling prophecies, for they will give you a clear indication of what's in store. But remember, they are not destined to happen. You can always change the conversation.

What conversation do you need to change?

JOURNAL:

Free Yourself from Old Ideas

The law that frees you is the same law that binds you. You create your life with the thoughts, attitudes, ideas, feelings, and beliefs that have become habitual patterns in your brain. Your old ideas have become the habitual patterns of thinking that are now running your life. As the saying goes, "Synapses that fire together, wire together."

However, you can be free from these old patterns. You can free yourself from your past by firing new synapses and wiring new pathways of thought and belief in your brain. This creates new habitual ways of thinking that build the life you choose for yourself.

Journal about the old patterns from which you choose to free yourself. Explore what you will replace them with.

JOURNAL:

July 21
Can't Help Emanating

You reveal yourself to others by the vibration of your consciousness. Life is not about getting, it's about giving. You are emanating all the time—you can't help it. Have you ever met a leader or teacher in whose presence you felt love or compassion? On the other hand, have you ever come across someone who gives you the creeps, someone who just did not feel clean? You bring to the neutral environment a vibe that is as real as your body.

You can be the emitter of Spirit's Presence as opposed to the bringer of worldly illusions. If you live in the Grace of God, you will be free of the cause and effect of others' third dimensional fallout. Your Good is not dependent on the favors of anyone. You cannot be deprived of your Good by anyone else's actions. A consciousness infused with Truth walks away from the creeps and brings to the party all that is necessary for a good life.

What creeps do you need to be walking away from?

JOURNAL:

Sculpting a Life

Everyday you think and dream, worry and plan. You go down those tracks over and over again because your thought patterns are familiar and comfortable. These repetitive thoughts become the mold for your subconscious mind to create the life you are living today. If you want to know what you are thinking, simply look at your life right now.

The good news is that, since you created this life you have now, you can create any life you want. You can keep the parts of this life you really like, and you can begin to shape a new mold with your thoughts and expectations that will bring about a new reality.

This is not much different than what a sculptor does with the clay— repeatedly shaping a curve, angle, or line, keeping each in proportion with the other. If something isn't quite right, the sculptor starts over, keeping what works and redoing what doesn't.

What kind of a life are you sculpting? What needs to be changed? What do you want to keep?

JOURNAL:

Who's Painting Your World

I was watching a painter standing before his canvas as he contemplated what colors to add and strokes to make to bring forth the brilliant greens of the jungle scene we were both admiring. Had I been painting the same scene on my own canvas at that moment, it wouldn't have looked anything like what the artist was painting. And that wouldn't have been the fault of the canvas! Obviously, the painting itself can't add or delete one touch of color. It can't improve or destroy anything on its own.

Our life, our body, and our world of affairs are like that canvas, which must respond to the creative direction given to it. It doesn't matter if what we are telling it is beautiful or ugly, brilliant or dull; the canvas will reproduce at the level of our participation. The spiritual law says that all effect is governed by mind.

On your canvas of life, you are given the first option. Are you going to do the painting as you see things, or are you going to give your brushes away and allow someone else to have at it?

JOURNAL:

Coloring in the Lines

Remember being taught to color in the lines? Remember when you learned that sky was blue, not green, and grass was green, not purple? The message was clear—there is a right way to do this. The other message was: be sure it looks real. In the process, your magical, imaginative, child-eyes were trained to see life in a certain way, and to create life in a certain way.

Yet, there is so much more going on than what you see with your eyes or hear with your ears. Practice seeing with your heart or listening with you hands. Practice looking through your intuition and feeling with your mind. Turn the normal way you approach things upside-down by using a different physical, mental, or emotional sense. Tune into your radical, altered perceptions. What's going on that you sense with your other senses—intuition, perception, awareness?

Give yourself permission to color outside the lines of your life.

JOURNAL:

The Keystone

A keystone is the final stone, the wedge that goes on top of an arch to lock all the other stones in place. It's the key that makes the difference by keeping the arch from collapsing. Yet, if any of the other stones in the arch were missing, the whole entrance would collapse.

Every aspect of your life has played an important and integral part in developing your character. No matter what it has been, it is a perfect and valuable piece of your structural make up. All the life experiences and lessons come together and make sense when God is the keystone and the cap that pulls it all together. Let Spirit rest in the crown position of your life.

Where would your perspective change if you realized God was the keystone of your life?

JOURNAL:

It's Coming Back

If love, caring, and compassion haven't shown up in your life, it's because you have not been casting the proper bread upon the sea. The bread on the water is allocated for those who send it forth. Life is like a bank account; you can't draw out what you haven't deposited.

It may not always be possible to change the circumstances going on around you, but you can change your relationship to and interpretation of them. Whether you send forth fear or understanding, it is multiplied and returned. It becomes the environment you inhabit. You are in an abundant universe, and abundance pours forth from within you. You get to draw forth from the infinite reservoir all that you want to cast upon the waters of life. So choose wisely—it's coming back.

What new "bread" do you wish to cast upon the water?

JOURNAL:

Where are you Looking?

If you ask tightrope walkers how they do it, they reply, "Always look forward and don't look down. The body goes where the eyes go." This is also true about your life. You go where you're looking. What you perceive, you receive. Where your attention goes, energy flows. What is filling your field of awareness? You can expect that which is before you to remain in your life until you change that which is filling your awareness. If you are looking back in your life, your past will follow you. If you are looking down, expect things to start heading that way.

The good news is that no matter where you find yourself—up or down, heaven or hell—Spirit has never left you. This means the Spiritual Principle which responds to your vision continues to be in operation, and you can use it to pull yourself through. Stop giving away your power, and take responsibility for where you are looking. Stop trying to find your freedom from the lure of this world, and come to know the freedom of seeing as God sees.

Where do you need to look in a different direction?

JOURNAL:

Whose Laundry is Dirty?

One morning, a man looked out the window and saw his new neighbor hanging laundry out to dry. He told his wife that their neighbor's laundry sure looked dirty. He told her that someone should give them washing lessons, or maybe they should try a different detergent. This went on for a few weeks until one morning, sitting down for breakfast, the husband noticed how clean his neighbor's laundry looked. When he told his wife that someone must have given them some laundry lessons, she smiled and told him that she had gotten up early that morning and washed the windows!

More often than not, it's your windows that need cleaning and not a problem that needs solving. You view life through your consciousness. If you are not seeing the presence of God everywhere you look, then it's a good indication there is something impairing your view.

What windows are you currently looking through that could use some cleaning?

JOURNAL:

Delaying the Delight

There is a Buddhist saying, "When love meets happiness, there is joy." When you live in the here and now, joy has a clear path for expression. When you attempt to get somewhere or achieve something for your happiness, you postpone joy. You delay the delight. Joy is necessary for enlightenment. To be a Light, you must move beyond the heaviness that you carry. What do you need to drop in order to be happy now?

Joy can be neither faked, nor contained. It is a soul experience that sparkles through your eyes and lights up a room. It is a turn-on to those who want lightness in their world. A joyously free and light consciousness reflects the many qualities attributed to God. This state of being is not dependent on outside happenings but rather on the transcendent inner realm of spiritual connectedness.

Where does love meet happiness in your world?

JOURNAL:

Divine Awareness

You are a point of consciousness through which God manifests Itself into form. When you look out from the God standpoint, you are living the Christ way. The good you do is your Divine nature shining through. When healing happens, it is the opening of consciousness to the God realization.

It's not that there aren't problems on the human level; it's that in the Presence of God, there are no challenges. You don't need mental arguments to get you to a place of wholeness. With practice, you can consciously enter the spiritual atmosphere. The shift in consciousness will facilitate the physical shift. Healing takes place in proportion to the degree of Divine awareness. Healing has nothing to do with the amount of religion you have. It is your spiritual connection that makes the difference.

JOURNAL:

Quiet the Dualistic Approach

On the material plane, there are two powers: a greater and a lesser. In the mental realm, there is a stronger and a lesser. When dealing in the material state of consciousness, the medical world has its benefits and can be a blessing to your state of health. As one moves into the mental realm, one tends to need less medical assistance, because awareness is more about mind over matter. This doesn't mean one is better than the other; they are just two different states of awareness.

As one moves into a greater conscious connection with the spiritual realm, the need for giving mental directives to the Law gives way to the Divine impress as your life. In the spiritual domain, there is no greater or lesser power. No one can use God. Only as you minimalize the dualistic approach can Spirit live through you. It appears as the wisdom that guides your thinking, the vision as to how you see, and the ability of your body. Let God appear and live as you, and you will know everything is already fine in all areas of your world.

What appears to have greater power in your life than God?

JOURNAL:

August

Freedom To Be

Joy is Contagious

Smile, and the whole world smiles back!

A baby chortling with glee can bring smiles to a whole room of people. In the same way, sharing your joy can lift the hearts of those around you. Simply walking around in your bliss makes you a magnet for and generator of joy. Your mental atmosphere colors the atmosphere of an entire room and can transform gloom and doom into hope and joy.

In the same manner you can to be lifted by another's joy. Surely, if even one person in the world is experiencing joy, you know that you can, too. Allowing someone's joy into your heart is like letting the rain fall on a parched garden. Revel in it and let it wash all over you.

In this manner, joy is shared and multiplied!

JOURNAL:

Happiness is Infectious

A new, scientific study has shown that a group of people is as happy as those who lead the group. When the leaders of a group become happier, so does everyone else. Likewise, people from one happy group impact the happiness of another group. It's like people are happiness infections!

Are you infecting people with happiness? Is your happiness contagious? Do you allow yourself to be infected with happiness?

JOURNAL:

August 3
The Best Medicine

Laughter comes in many sizes and sounds. There is the guffaw, the howl, the chortle, a chuckle, the hee-hee delight, the twitter of glee, and many others. Then, there's the belly laugh—the most healing of all.

Explore your laughter. In which kind of laughter do you indulge? When do you laugh? How often do you laugh? When was the last time your really belly laughed until the tears ran down you face?

JOURNAL:

A Feel-Good Experience

Western religion can be so serious. It seems to be about control, rules, and a code of ethics. There are writers who talk about being drunk on God. There are laughing Buddhas. The animal kingdom is full of God's creatures who know how to have fun. Why not bring fun and a sense of humor to your approach to life? Just because others want to be weighed down in seriousness on their way to God doesn't mean you have to be. If joy is not in your life, you might want to think about changing paths. You can always choose whether or not to be lifted up in the lightness of God.

Humor and laughter are a lot of fun to be around. Smiling doesn't equate to ungodly anymore than serious equates to spiritual. Don't you feel the joy of Spirit when you are around people who make you feel good? God is a feel-good experience. Laughter is a great elixir for healing whatever ails you. The places where you smile and laugh are those where you'll probably find God.

Instead of watching the news this evening, watch a comedy and laugh yourself to sleep.

JOURNAL:

Just for the Fun of It

One day, I realized that I had become obsessed with accomplishing, achieving, and growing in my life. I took everything I did as an opportunity to improve myself. I discovered that this was making me tired and cranky. So, I decided I would find something that I really enjoyed doing without trying to achieve anything other than enjoying it.

I started to grow herbs. Though the people I know who grow herbs always dry them, store them, and make them into tinctures, sachets, or oils, the idea of all that work overwhelmed and tired me. I simply wanted to grow them. I wanted to look at them, smell them, and crunch the leaves between my fingers. Every once in a while I may want to pick some for my cooking, but I really didn't care if I did anything with them or not. I wanted to grow herbs just for the fun of it.

I've invited many people, especially perfectionists and overachievers, to do a thing just for the fun of it—some activity that they will not try to improve, accomplish, or make into a new career. One friend joined the choir, another took up knitting. The friend in the choir will never sing a solo; she just does it for fun. My friend who knits has so much fun unraveling what she knits that she buys yarn, but doesn't buy any patterns.

What do you do just for the fun of it?

JOURNAL:

Finding Humor in Your Life

Often, the only saving grace to a situation is finding the humor in it. Learning to laugh at yourself, your reactions, and behavior can help diffuse the seriousness of many situations. This doesn't mean that you ridicule or shame yourself. It means that you allow yourself to be tickled by the silliness in which humans can get caught up. You allow yourself to find the ridiculousness in a situation, not a person. You invite the comical side of life to help you not get stuck or take things too personally.

Do you like to tell funny stories about yourself or do you only tell them about others? Do you see the humor in your own seriousness?

Explore what it would take for you to bring more lightness and light-heartedness into you life. How would that feel?

JOURNAL:

Inner Interests

The more in tune you are with your inner interests, the clearer your direction in life is. Many spiritual people say you should have no desire. How boring would that be? Though it's nice to just bliss out and do nothing for a while, you are here to be an expression of life made manifest, just so long as your walk through this world isn't leaving a wake of harm or a giant footprint on someone or something. How exciting it is to be in a co-creative relationship with Spirit!

To live a suppressed and unexpressed life is sad. Don't be held back by false spiritual perspectives that somehow say it's holier not to be happy. Go for life full out! When your joy level dwindles, don't think it's the end of the world. You are now free to redirect your life force. Don't be attached to an outcome; rather, experience the joy of creative energies moving through you in new ways. When you are alive with Spirit, there is no room for anything else.

How can you honor your interests in your world more?

JOURNAL:

Freedom to Play

So many great inventions were created through the simple act of playing with ideas, possibilities, objects, and plans. Who said life had to be so serious? Play is refreshing, exuberating, relaxing, and just plain fun. Play isn't just for kids; it's for the kid in all of us.

You have Eternity and Infinity as your playground. You have the freedom to create your life. Why not create a life that you enjoy?

What do you like to do that has no goal, no need for improvement, no results, and no purpose other than the sheer fun and joy of it? Give yourself permission and freedom to play!

JOURNAL:

Playing the Game of Life

What kind of games do you remember playing as a kid? Did you only play sports or board games that had winners and losers? Or did you play games that were sheer outpourings of imagination, like dress up, Legos, or jump rope?

When you play the game of life, do you keep score, thinking of it as a game with winners and losers? What if you played it like dress up or jump rope, or simply making fun shapes in the sandbox?

Life is your sandbox, in which you get to create anything you want. You can dress up and make believe whatever you like. There are no winner and losers. There are only people who play and those who don't. Which kind are you?

JOURNAL:

Long Summer Nights

Do you remember those long summer nights of playing kick-the-can or hide-and-go-seek until it was so dark that no one could see anyone else? Do you remember ignoring your mother's call to come in because you wanted to squeeze one more drop of fun out of the long summer day? How full and rich life was, and how precious each moment was! You didn't want to go to bed for fear of missing anything, and you couldn't wait to get up in the morning to start playing again.

Are you still squeezing every drop of life out of your days? Are you going to bed each night with an I-can't-wait-for-tomorrow kind of a feeling? If not, why not? What would it take for your life to become like that in the midst of your adult reality?

JOURNAL:

Connecting with Your Inner Child

Everyone has an inner child. Your inner child still sees the world through a child's eyes and with a child's comprehension. Your inner child is delighted when you remember to play, laugh, be in wonder, and live in the magical mystery of life. If these ways of being are not apparent to you, you may want to invite your inner child out to play. Ask him or her how old she is and what he likes to do. Tell the child that it's okay to play now, because you will keep him or her safe and protected.

Sometimes, though, your inner child pops out in a business setting, a committed relationship, or in matters of money. The problem is that your inner child does not know how to behave or make decisions in the adult world. The child gets frightened or angry, and then reacts exactly as if he or she was on the playground at recess. If your inner child is running your life in a direction you don't want, you can invite the child back into the safety of your arms. Tell your inner child that you will take care of things so he or she doesn't need to, and that you will protect him or her and provide everything she or he didn't get from your parents.

This allows you, and not your inner child, to be in charge of your life. When do you want to bring your child out to play?

JOURNAL:

Freedom to Be

Take the time to simply be. Be you. Be who you are, just as you are. Let yourself enjoy the freedom of simply being.

Yes, you still need to grow. Yes, there are more things to do. However, there is the need to just be.

Explore your ability to be. Then practice it.

JOURNAL:

Sitting in the Shade

There's nothing better on a warm summer day than to sit in the shade with a good book. It's relaxing and refreshing, and it restores equilibrium to a busy life. Time to sit, time to simply be, time to rest—these are as important as your commitment to accomplish, your intention to grow, and your willingness to become.

Taking the time to simply be allows you to reflect on how far you've come and what is already wonderful in your life. This time lets you see that God is always present, love is flourishing, and life is growing. You can relax and enjoy the fruits of your labors.

What do you do, like sitting in the shade, that restores your soul and lets you be at peace with yourself?

JOURNAL:

Dishwashing to God

Brother Lawrence made dishwashing an acceptable approach to Spirit. Raking leaves can do it also, as can housecleaning. Have you ever made a bed so mindfully that the next person to sleep in it would feel the consciousness it was prepared with? Did you tuck in the covers as if a saint was going to be sleeping there? Simple, rhythmic tasks can take you to God, moving you from the thinking side of your brain to the receptive side, where inspiration and insight are received.

What would it take for you to just be? What can you do to quiet your mind, allowing Spirit to come to you in ways you couldn't have humanly planned? Your descriptive words can give way to actual awareness, where God-consciousness emerges through you, and the revelation of it as your Infinite Being frees you from worldly constraints.

JOURNAL:

Busy, Busy, Busy

Where in your life are you too busy to have time for the Truth? It seems to be generally accepted that being overly busy is a respectable and responsible way to be in our society. Well, it's overrated! Your mind has the uncanny ability to distort the importance of your business to the point where you actually believe it is right and that your frazzled feelings are wrong. It can convince you that none of your activities can be sacrificed and that there is a to-do list just waiting for a time slot to open up in your life.

Remember to check in and see if this is how you want to be feeling on the inside, not to think about what you are going to do next. Do you have enough time in your busy life just to be? When you relax into the Spirit of your being, life is no longer misallocated by looking for satisfaction and fulfillment in your doing, because it will be realized in the midst of your being.

Where in your life can your reallocate some time to just be?

JOURNAL:

Relax

Stress reduction classes are as popular in medical circles these days as they used to be in spiritual circles. Yet, the point is not meditation or yoga; it's stillness, silence, emptiness, and tranquility.

When the mind is quiet, free from thoughts, concerns or memories, there is profound silence. In this silence, you don't need to "get" anything; you just be. Relax, and allow your body to do its natural, healing, regenerative processes without any concern from you. Enter the solitude, but not to get away or experience relief from anything. You'll be amazed how much better you will feel when you set aside some time everyday to be quiet without expectation.

What's keeping you from closing your eyes for five minutes right now? What's more important than your peace and inner balance?

JOURNAL:

Vacations are Medicinal

In Europe, everyone has six weeks off for vacation, and they take all six weeks! Vacation is an extended period of time during which you relax enough to break out of your ruts and routines. Do you take your vacation time?

When you explore the freedom to joyously create whatever life you want, taking a vacation gives you practice in the very skills you need. Vacations are opportunities to completely get out of your routine. They offer you a different view on life by taking you someplace else and doing things that are completely different from what you normally do every day. This breaks up places where you may be stuck in your thinking and doing. When you come back from vacation, you are better equipped to see and engage your everyday life in the same way you engaged during your vacation.

When are you taking your next vacation? Where are you going, and what will you do? Enjoy! This medicine is not only good for you; it tastes and feels great!

JOURNAL:

Rest and Emergence

Pelicans dive and catch their lunch from the ocean's edge. Then they lift their large bodies out of the water and take flight with their prize. This can be like doing your spiritual work. You dive in for your spiritual nourishment, and then use that power to lift off from where you are. It might take some time to accumulate the necessary lift-off power. As comfortable as your present level may be, when you finally do lift off, you will then see other promises to investigate.

Rest and emergence are natural parts of the path. What's important is to neither burn out and crash, nor relax and become fat. Life is a balance between going out and coming in. It's the momentum that moves you along your journey, revealing new scenery that encourages your progress. Enjoy the new, allowing the energy to build for your next lift-off.

Where do you feel energy gathering in your life for the next lift-off?

JOURNAL:

Sabbath Time

In the Hebrew culture, many rules developed around the Sabbath. These rules were designed to help people refrain from any work on that day, so they could spend it contemplating God, being with their families, and taking a needed rest. While the rules aren't that important, the idea of a Sabbath is.

Taking time for the Sabbath means setting aside the things you are working on that simply keep you busy. You consciously decide to rest, relax, and enjoy some quiet downtime. This may include being with others, but most likely not in a party or other loud, crowded atmosphere.

The idea of the Sabbath is to renew yourself, restore your inner balance, and create space in your life. Journal about creating more Sabbath time. What would that look like? Then, go put it in your calendar.

JOURNAL:

Space for Joy

It is challenging to experience joy when you are overworked, exhausted, or simply too busy. Creating time and space for rest, play, rejuvenation, and simply doing nothing at all brings balance into your life. It makes space for Joy.

You may have a story about how hard you work, how many demands and people are pulling on you, or how little time you have. These stories simply perpetuate the lack of balance in your life.

What new story do you want to tell about yourself and your life? What do you need to change to make the new story a reality? Make space for Joy in your life today. You deserve it!

JOURNAL:

Porch-sitting

Americans used to sit on the front porch and watch their neighbors walk by. This invited casual conversation, friendship among diverse people, and a sense of belonging in the community. Porch-sitting fosters the idea of backdoor friends. These are the people who walk into the back door of your house without knocking, sit down at the kitchen table for pie and coffee without an invitation, and are always welcome in your life.

Spirit shows up in your life as all kinds of people interacting with you at all kinds of levels. From your best friend to the clerk at the store, everyone is the face of God with a gift to give.

Explore where and with whom you are developing acquaintances and friendships. Journal about the times when you are closed down or shut off and why that might be.

JOURNAL:

Demand for Your Attention

Is there a place in your life that demands your full attention. These places are like driving on a twisting, turning mountain road where you have to keep slowing down to navigate the next bend of highway— you never know what is waiting around the next curve. On one side of the car, the scenery varies between a mountain wall and picturesque mountain landscape; on the other side is a perilous cliff with breathtaking views. Even if there are others in the car commenting on the spectacular scenery, you don't want to take your eyes off the road for a second.

Life can be like that road trip through the mountains with its twists and turns. You never quite know what tomorrow holds. Today has its beauty and gifts, yet demands your attention to speed up and slow down through the curves of life. Remember, you can pull over any time to appreciate where you are and breath in the wonder that surrounds you. When you feel the pressures or tensions of this world start to mount, pull over to the side, get off the main thoroughfare, breathe in, and realize you are in God's country.

Where in your world would you benefit from pulling over and taking a breath?

JOURNAL:

August 23

Stop Picking At It

Once good things start showing up in your life, don't interrupt them! This is a magical time when the gates open and abundance starts accumulating. Be in a state of appreciation and awe. Spiritual practice takes patience; it can seem like nothing is going on at first. When you notice your world working with calm trust instead of amp-out force, you have entered a new dimension in consciousness.

The quickest way to pull yourself out of Creation is to start waiting for the other shoe to drop. When this happens, you have to continue knowing that Good is only the seed of Power yet to be. Self-cultivation accumulates energy. The way to sidetrack the momentum is to question, rather than trust. So stop picking away at what's working. You did the work—now enjoy it.

Where are you interfering with the Good in your life?

JOURNAL:

Spiritual Time

The Buddha taught taking one hour a day, one day a week, one week a month, and one month a year as spiritual time. Jesus expounded upon the Jewish Sabbath time by reminding people that it's not about slavishly following rules, but about regularly setting time aside to be with God. All the great spiritual teachers remind you to regularly set aside time in which you attend to and contemplate your spiritual nature.

This time can't be hurried or forced. Your spiritual discipline helps you set a specific time aside to be available to the Presence, but it does not guarantee it. You court the Presence the way you might coax a kitten into your hand.

Find that quiet time to spend with your God, and God will spend time with you.

JOURNAL:

Smile Meditation

I found the following mediation in the book *Eat, Pray, Love*, by Elizabeth Gilbert. I have enjoyed using it, and I pass it on to you.

When you sit in your mediation, simply focus on bringing a small smile to your lips. Then, focus on smiling in your heart. Then, focus on smiling in your liver. Repeat this cycle over and over again. When you find yourself wandering off, bring yourself back to the smile on your lips, and begin again.

After you've explored this for a while, write down your thoughts and feelings.

JOURNAL:

The Instinctive Side

I watched three deer, brilliant in their beauty, stroll through the woods. The woods provide their food, protection, and playground. They didn't need classes on how to live in nature. They intuitively know how to live because of their connection with the Life Force. Their thinking minds didn't separate them from the flow.

Your rational mind can separate you from the instinctive side of life. The truth is, all you'll ever need is provided in your forest. You might have buildings reaching to the sky instead of trees, and stores in which to find your food instead of hillsides, yet it is your forest. This is the time and place for you to be in the flow of Life. Spirit's currents will guide you through streets as naturally as it will down rivers. Spirit is as omnipresent and fully available for you as it is for a deer in the forest.

How have you been denying your connection with the flow?

JOURNAL:

The River

Standing alongside a river, you don't need much imagination to realize that the river is constantly new. By putting your hand or body in it, you'll know that its currents and rushing beauty are in constant motion. You cannot step into the same river twice.

The flow of Spirit, with its richness, beauty, and strength, waits for you to step into Its magnificent movement. Expression is not stagnant. The power and potential of the Divine has always been there—moving. You can look back at history to see where it has run and cut its course through time. Yet, it beckons you today to come play at the river's edge, swim with its currents, and know for yourself, through experience, the joy of being in the flow.

What's keeping you from jumping in?

JOURNAL:

Riptide for Good

Sometimes when you get caught in the riptides of life, you just have to let go and go with the flow. In the ocean, when a strong undertow gets you and you are being sucked out from shore, you'll exhaust your human strength by attempting to swim against it. The common wisdom says to relax and let it pull you out past the turbulence, where you can swim parallel to shore and come back in where it's calmer.

It takes a lot of trust to ride out the currents going in the opposite direction of your apparent safety. Is there anywhere in your life you have exhausted your human energy attempting to get back to "solid ground?" Sometimes in life, you have to use the power of the undercurrents to sweep you through the tumultuous waves of life. Stop fighting and know the forces at hand will deliver you to a clear opening for your Good.

JOURNAL:

Harmony Is

Spiritual growth is not based on how many classes you've taken or how many years you've engaged in spiritual practices. Nor is it based on the number of advanced trainings you've been involved in facilitating. Rather, spiritual growth is a sense of harmony in your human affairs, with no great, emotional roller coaster or fluctuation in facing the human condition. This kind of harmony is not based on outcome or income. It is the natural, spiritual state. Our spiritual identity is not based on changing, correcting, or manifesting anything in this world of form. All discord is a belief that you have a life separate from God.

Harmony is. Not will be or can be—it *is*. Any sense of separation exists merely as an illusion. If a client were to tell me that he had fish scales growing all over his body, I wouldn't pray to remove the scales, but rather for the client to awaken to the Truth of his true identity. In this type of realization, one comes to know he never had fish scales, or cancer, or lack, or limitation of any kind. These kinds of limiting ideas are only possible with an untrue sense of a self that is apart from the True Source. As long as we fight the illusion, there is conflict. The sooner one enters the all pervasive consciousness that is Harmony, then Harmony is the experience.

JOURNAL:

Time to Hook Up

Prayer used to be a larger part of everyday life. We prayed at church services on Sundays and Wednesday nights, before meals, before going to sleep, and then again at the start of the day. After dinner, many families used to gather for a spiritual reading and conversation. Now, it seems people either go out to hook up with others or plug into their electronic world by themselves. Your spirituality shouldn't be one more thing on your to-do list, but something that is woven throughout your everyday life.

Reflect on last week and count how many times you stopped to hook up with your Higher Power. Were there too many to count? If not, then reassess this upcoming week and see how many places you can find in each day to remember your Source.

JOURNAL:

Reflections at Dawn

It is awesome to sit among ancient pines and reflect on an idyllic lake surrounded by majestic mountains reaching toward a big, blue sky at dawn. Endless beauty leaves no question about the givingness of Life. Nature is prolific in its constant offering. Flow is its natural state, ever moving from one season to the next. Anything that remains at rest, stagnates. Nature is always available for you to step into its richness. Just as long as you don't try to own it, you can always be part of it all.

As soon as you attempt to cut out a piece and hold on to it, you start limiting your experience of that which is Infinite. The desire to get more becomes a driving and self-limiting force. To live in the flow is to constantly pour forth that which you are. You are an abundant expression of Spirit, an outlet for the outpouring of the ever-expanding Good. The more you experience, the more you have to give; the more you give, the more comes to you and flows through you.

What are you holding on to and what do you have to give?

JOURNAL:

September

Free to Learn and Grow

September 1-8
The Joy of Earth School

September 9-19
The Joy of Trusting Your Teachers

September 20-24
Joyous Peace

September 25-30
The Joy of Spiritual Growth

Earth School

Do you remember the smells of your first day of school? Remember sharpening your pencils and getting your supplies organized? Remember being excited and nervous, all at the same time?

This lifetime is your Earth School. Every year, you move to the next level and learn something new. What supplies are you bringing with you to school these days? Are they cared for and handy or lost in a habit of unconsciousness?

Take the time to list and prepare the supplies you need for this level of Earth School.

JOURNAL:

Service: The Price of Passage

We are so blessed to be passing through this time and space, having accepted the invitation to learn our lessons in this Eden of a classroom. Souls are lined up for this incarnation, and we are the chosen guests in this world where we have been offered all the necessary abundance to move with ease and grace. Let us not forget to give back in ways of service to make this world a better place. Service is love in action, and there's a big difference between "I should have done it" and "I did it."

Sacred service does not come from obligation. Rather, it leaves behind a sweet scent of humility and appreciation for having had the opportunity to contribute. When you find it in your heart to reach out beyond your personal world of concerns, you get the gift of being fully present in the moment. True service doesn't look for compensation or headlines. The joy of the experience is more than enough. You don't have to wait until the end of the journey to enjoy the blessings of this world. Service is the language of the heart and the passage you give for this life.

JOURNAL:

Signing Up

In high school and college, you are expected to register for core classes, but you also have a wonderful opportunity to sign up for electives. Do you remember excitedly asking your friends what electives they were going to take this year?

What core classes have you signed up for in the school of your life? Forgiveness? Unconditional Love? Discovering the power of your word? Learning to ask for what you want? Joyous Living? Freedom from Fear? Have you completed these classes? What do you have to keep signing up for again and again? What new core classes do you want to take?

Are you taking electives that interest you? What are you learning and doing just for the fun of it? Are you letting yourself play in different areas of your life without worrying about whether you pass or fail?

JOURNAL:

Beginner's Mind

Zen Buddhism features the concept of "beginner's mind." This is the state of not knowing anything about the subject in front of you, knowing you don't know, and being completely open to seeing, discovering, and learning something for the very first time.

This is the perfect state in which to learn. It is also a wonderful state of mind from which to approach areas of your life in which you have become stuck, unthinking, or frustrated.

If you had no preconceived ideas at all and simply allowed these areas to show themselves to you, what would you discover that is new? What might you learn about handling it differently?

It's always good to practice "beginner's mind" in any area of your life.

JOURNAL:

From Belief to Experiencing

Believing in something is a good place to start, but it's only the beginning. Believing there is a continent called Australia is a nice start, but it doesn't get you there. You still have a long journey to embark upon to really know Australia. It's nice to believe in the Spiritual Kingdom, but that doesn't get you there, either. You must move from belief to experience.

The next part of the journey is to experience the causative factors which bring form into your reality. With that realization, you become blessed by all the good those discoveries bring. You realize they are always there for you. You cannot bribe Spirit into being more, nor can you mess up so badly Spirit would withdraw any aspect of Its allness. You come to know the Kingdom through experience beyond belief, and to see that you are the one who blocks or starts the flow of Divine Grace into your life.

Where in your life would you like to move from believing to experiencing?

JOURNAL:

Remembering How to Learn

As a child, you were constantly learning. You learned how to walk by falling down. You learned how to speak by imitating others. You learned how to ride a bicycle with training wheels. You learned how to throw a ball by practicing. These are normal and natural processes for children.

As an adolescent, you may have learned that learning is awkward. You practiced driving a car, and that might have been scary. You learned about holding hands and kissing, and that could have been awkward. Sometimes trying new things was exciting, and other times people laughed at you.

Most adults have completely forgotten how to learn. Because we may have felt awkward trying something new, we made the mistaken assumption that we can't do it, aren't good at it, or that it isn't meant for us to learn.

Get in touch with all the ways you learned as a child. What are you willing to learn, so that you can practice the art of learning?

JOURNAL:

Talk About it or Experience It

Have you ever had anyone ask, "How can you believe in God?" They imply that you seem too intelligent for that kind of stuff. For some stoic and philosophical thinkers, a Higher Power is like a fairy tale. But taking a walk in nature, leaving the rational thinker behind, you'll experience the ineffable. There's no need to describe your experience. You can talk about a stroll through nature or you can just go walk in it. There is a huge difference between talking about God and experiencing God.

Let the over-analytical ones wrestle over the impossible constructs of Spirit, while you step outside and feel the whispering winds brush against your face. Arguing doesn't penetrate the realm of Spirit. Reasoning faculties remain in the three-dimensional world, where they can be constructive or destructive. Once you pierce the veil and see into that kind of Power and Presence, you'll come to realize it is not a power and presence from a material sense or human standpoint. It's a Presence not because It has a form, but because you can feel It just as the illumined have over the ages. It's a Power because peace now lives where there was once conflict. It's not a power over anything, but just because there is nothing else.

Let others argue for their limitations and their lonely walks through life, while you feel the love of Life knowing Itself as you.

JOURNAL:

Out of Bounds

When you go "out of bounds" in a game, you have gone outside the agreed upon play area. There are times to color outside the lines or to stretch the rules, but not when you have made an agreement about what the rules are. The sidelines of life are for observers. The action and excitement are in the game. Stop contemplating how things should be. Take off your warm-up suit and step into the arena. You made an agreement to the manifesting laws of Cause and Effect when you came into this world.

Life is fun! Life is interactive. Life is an active dynamic in which you can move beyond the concept of opposing forces toward that of pure power. There is no Divine law that supports opposing teams; there is no bigger than or less than. There is no one or no thing to overcome. The opponents in the game are made real by the thoughts we project—Cause and Effect. The only way you'll ever really know how this law works is to get off the theoretical bench and have life echo back your projected meanings, so you can actually have interaction in which you learn through firsthand experience.

Where do you need to pay greater attention to see how your projections are being echoed back?

JOURNAL:

Becoming Teachable

Being teachable means that you are open to new ideas—you are aware that there is more to learn than you ever imagined. Looking at things in a new way, continuing to explore possibilities, and being willing to be surprised are the hallmarks of someone who is teachable.

Are you teachable? In what areas of your life are you willing to learn something completely new? Are you willing to be surprised? Are you willing to explore things from a different angle?

JOURNAL:

They're Everywhere

Some of the great spiritual teachers who walked this planet didn't consider themselves great at all. They tended to see themselves as servants of Spirit. They didn't go about glorifying themselves in their own time. Their humility was part of their greatness. Their immortalization came as others recollected their great teachings and healings.

These people were instruments through which the Divine was revealed. They were transparent channels and conduits for God to be made manifest. They allowed Spirit to be the Allness of their being, and were guided by that. There was a time when ministers had to be dressed in flowing robes to be recognized. Today, there is no need to identify the God expressions walking in this world by their dress, just by their emanations of light and joy. If you look and listen, you'll find them everywhere—in business suits or swimsuits, pants or skirts, driving a truck or a Porsche, and maybe just walking their dog. Pay attention—they are all around.

What great spiritual teachers have surprised you by their costumes, and what did they teach you?

JOURNAL:

Finding Your Teacher

Eastern spiritual traditions put a great deal of emphasis on finding a teacher or guru. The student or disciple then willingly puts themselves into the hands of the teacher or guru as a way to grow and learn. This relationship can provide a wonderful opening and deepening of spirituality. In the wrong hands, though, it can be a recipe for real trouble.

You may not find yourself called to having a guru, but there may be real value in aligning yourself with a spiritual teacher. Things to look for in a teacher are: the desire to see you grow beyond what they can teach you; humility and openness; less of a need for them to be right as for you to be learning; and a deep respect and belief in your Divinity, not just theirs. You will know when you no longer need that person as your teacher.

When you find someone who can be a teacher for you, be willing to be challenged, comforted, stretched, expanded, and celebrated.

JOURNAL:

Teachers in the Park

When you are open and receptive, you find that life is full of teachers. As a child, I would join my dad on his visits to the shoeshine guy in the kiosk at the park. Though my father could shine his own shoes, I realized he found something in this rapt exchange of worlds with the shoeshine guy that included wisdom, humor, and good listening. Somehow, there was a clearer perspective of personal and global events being conveyed.

I, too, gained insight from observing and conversing with those in the park. I learned joy from the children playing on the swings and in the sandbox. I observed the importance of friendship from seeing the mothers talking and sharing whatever it is moms talk about. I saw trust and cooperation going on in the basketball games. I noticed the dedication of coaches and the support of cheering parents. I learned about caring for the earth from the gardeners and grounds keepers, beauty from the flowers, and seasons and cycles from the trees. I learned respect for elders sitting in the sun and playing checkers.

These were my teachers in the park who were walking their talk without even knowing it. Who are some of your unlikely teachers, and what do they reveal to you?

JOURNAL:

Your Spirituality

When someone says, "Follow me on the spiritual path; I've got the answer," it's often a good time to run the other way. Spirituality is a personal experience, not an exclusive one. Being a student of truth, an explorer of wisdom, and a practitioner of compassion are life-long projects that take twists and turns on the spiritual path. As long as you are in this world, there is always more to understand about your true nature. It is not wise to give away your power to anyone or anything outside of you. Put your trust in the teachings of Universal Truth, not teachers.

Religion is about belonging, proper protocols, and shared values. In your exploration for spiritual understanding, remain inquisitive, open, and curious about how God shows up in every moment of your life. You came from the One, and you don't need a go-between for the Divine connection. Spirituality is about everyday awareness of the Presence as your life.

JOURNAL:

Leadership

Leaders are most effective when they are in tune with their environments. It is more powerful to have been in the trenches than to have a lot of book training. Invaluable leadership means having the eyes to see what's emerging, the courage to point out the direction, and the respect of others to get on board.

A leader must have the conviction to commit and the ability to communicate that commitment. A good leader conveys vision, joy, and enthusiasm to a project. Grouches make people want to quit. Confident leaders invite the frontline folks into the design process to help create the architecture for success. Someone who welcomes opposing points of view, passionate arguments, and criticism without taking it personally is invaluable when it comes to structuring a new direction. Then when it's rolled out, it has the buy-in because of the shared leadership.

What qualities of leadership do you appreciate?

JOURNAL:

September 15
Spiritual Snobbery

Is your spirituality a form of snobbery? There are those who profess to know so much about spirituality that they make new spiritual explorers feel less than whole. Being in the presence of spiritual snobs doesn't impart a feel-good experience; it's more like a trial with a judge and jury. You can't even point this out to them, because then they'd say you don't have "it," whatever "it" is. They would also quickly ask, "How did you create that experience for yourself?"

When you have a conscious connection with God, life fulfills according to Divine Plan, not according to the outlines and dictates of false spiritual authority. What's interesting is that the higher plan for you always turns out much better and more fun than others would have you believe. People can point to the moon, but they can't give you the experience of it. Others can point you in a direction, but the journey is yours. It doesn't need to include people who attempt to make others feel lessthan. Besides, why would you want to know someone who would have you behave in such a disempowering manner?

What snobs do you need to drop from your world?

JOURNAL:

Your Living Room

God doesn't talk to you any more clearly if you're starving in an ashram in India, freezing in a Tibetan monastery, or comfortably sitting in your own living room. Your true essence comes from within, right where you are. Flowers may not be as beautiful in their early stages, but they don't need to be in the country to blossom. They will bloom where they are planted. It's when they finally open up that they let out their fragrance and colors.

You cannot rush a flower into its attractiveness, nor can you rush your unfoldment. Trust your center and know what's there even before the world sees it. It's the God-seed of your being that leads you toward your spiritual awakening. The fears and doubts you entertain may hold you back for awhile, but relax and know what's at your center. The more you understand what is inside you, the more the arrogance of this world will dissolve. Allow your consciousness to draw from the nourishment of the love, peace, abundance, and joy that are present in your living room right now.

What is at your center that you haven't shown the world yet?

JOURNAL:

Bloom Where Planted

Sometimes a new life seems to be calling us. But is it really? The most useful question to ask yourself is, "Are you running to something or running from something?" If you are running to something, then, by all means, set your intention, take the plunge, and go for it.

Sometimes, however, what we really want to do is run from something. Yet we know that wherever we go, there we are. Perhaps this is the time to stay put and use this opportunity to grow. As we grow, we bloom in unexpected ways—giving up old stories, letting go of old beliefs, no longer re-creating the same old situations. When this is true, we can bloom right where we are planted.

JOURNAL:

What Does it Mean

What good does it do you to have visions, yet not know what they mean? What is the value of seeing beyond the physical and not knowing what you see? You have to understand what you receive for it to have any relevance in your life. Wouldn't it be nice to have as much clarity as biblical Joseph when it comes to interpreting your dreams?

Wisdom comes when you pay attention. Let the first go-round teach you what it means. You will become aligned with the Real and be able to delineate the difference between the speaking of imagination and that of Spirit. There is only One Mind in which all is known, and there is no reason why you shouldn't be "in the know."

What visions have you had that still linger in your memory? Take them into the silence and request a current understanding.

JOURNAL:

Practitioners of Perfection

Are you someone who goes by the spirit of things or by the rules? A spiritual cliché asks: "Do you go by the letter of the law or the spirit of the law?" Are you caught up in doing "it" right, or how you *feel* while doing "it"? Is it about the beauty of the experience or doing it correctly? Practitioners of perfection often enjoy pointing out how you might want to try their way, so you can get "it" right.

When you are so concerned about getting it right that the joy goes out of the practice, it's time to take a look at your motive. Sometimes the intimidator is in your head. You do not come into your God-realization in a single moment. Although you have mystical experiences that can become filters of recollection, you still live with your feet in this world. If you were perfect, you wouldn't be here. So, be kind to yourself in your evolutionary process.

Where in your growth process can you be kinder?

JOURNAL:

No Fences

As I watched a gaggle of geese leading their goslings across the front lawn and under the split-rail fence into the neighbor's yard, it was clear to me that ducks don't understand the purpose of fences. They don't seem to get the concepts of "this is mine and this is yours" and "stay on your side." Somehow, they know you can't divvy up the territory. It all belongs to God, and owning the land just doesn't register with them.

Imagine taking down the fences and defenses that keep you in and people out. What would it be like to wander into your neighbor's yard without having to go through gates, everyone showing mutual respect and appreciation toward life and nature? Is it possible to trust others without the fear of being taken advantage of?

It all begins with knowing that you are trustworthy and respectful. Are you?

JOURNAL:

World Peace Day

Today has become known as an International Day of Peace. It's a day when the United Nations calls all nations to a worldwide observance of a 24-hour ceasefire. To begin this day, the Peace Bell, cast from coins donated by children from all the continents, is rung.

Do you commit today to a ceasefire from any warring or violent thoughts or nasty actions? Are you free enough from the dictates of your emotions and historical remembrances of pain to practice non-violence in thought and action for 24 hours? Feel the joy of walking through some of the minefields—and *mind* fields—of your consciousness, and know you are safe. Maybe you'll come to discover something new and wonderful about your enemies that could change your life.

Where in your life do you find yourself engaged in less than kind energy? Are you willing to have today be a place of neutrality? What can you do to ensure this practice?

JOURNAL:

Evolutionary Spirituality

All of life is evolving and has been for 14 billion years. There is an inner impulsion and guidance that universally evolves all of creation. Each new evolutionary thrust contains what which came before it, while at the same time creating something wholly new.

This evolutionary process is the unfolding of God as It expresses Its own infinite nature through an infinitely evolving creation. The wisdom and intelligence of the Universe is this Divine Infinite Reality showing up as all creation. In this process, life emerges out of Life, always growing, expanding, exploring, and expressing more of Itself.

Your life, in all its growth and evolution, is a part of this process. You are designed to evolve spiritually, emotionally, mentally, and physically. Explore the areas of your life where you are evolving. Is there a place where you are stuck?

JOURNAL:

Equinox and Equilibrium

Balance is the mid-point between extremes. It is here where day and night have the same length. It is here where rest and work, play and discipline, feasting and fasting come into harmony.

Finding equilibrium does not mean standing still between two extremes, but rather finding the way to balance them. Imagine it like a teeter-totter. The fun isn't in standing in the middle, trying to keep both sides perfectly even. The fun comes from moving from side to side, never banging either side too hard on the ground or getting one side stuck in the air.

Thus, you find that balance comes from having both rest and work in your life, both play and discipline. It means you know when it's time to feast and when it's time to fast.

Where are you out of balance in your life? Where are you comfortable with your equilibrium?

JOURNAL:

God's Not Listening

There is no "outside" God listening to you. The heavens will not punish you or reward you. Don't give thanks to some distant deity when standing in awe of the majestic beauty that lies before you. Instead, be filled with appreciation for Life Itself, which is being experienced in the moment as you. In your intuitive receptivity, be open to the all-knowingness that is ever available. This guidance won't let you down, because it is always present. Don't be fooled into thinking your good is dependent upon some outside entity bestowing its favor upon you. Though your spiritual evolution is to know there is not an "outside" God directing things, you should still act in integrity as if there were. Life responds to your level of consciousness, not because God is watching, but because of the immutable Law reflecting back to you what you have sent out.

What do you think about that?

JOURNAL:

It's Not as I Planned

It takes a strong connection to Source to persevere after defeat or setback without embracing the sense of "I failed." When you experience disappointment, you view life from the human level. Sometimes it is important to go through the range of emotions around experiences in your life, but when you are done with those feelings, drop them and choose to see as God sees. Maybe you are a business person who hasn't put a deal together for a year. It doesn't mean you are a failure; all it means is you haven't put a deal together for a year. Or maybe your prayers for healing haven't panned out like you wanted. It doesn't mean healing isn't going on; all it means is that the healing looks different than you planned. Sometimes, even death can be considered a perfect healing.

Give all you have to what you are doing and where you are headed, yet, surrender your addiction to how it must turn out for you to feel joyful. Allow Spirit to pour forth Its glory through all you do and you will come to know your connection when you are in the Valley of the Shadow of Death, as well as on the highest mountain top.

When did apparent failure give you a gift?

JOURNAL:

Interpretation is Yours

Fires occasionally burn the brush of Southern California, destroying thousands of acres, devouring homes and everything in their paths. Is this bad luck, bad karma, or an angry God? If you pay attention to what you think, you will receive a lot of clarity about your belief systems.

The easterly winds have been blowing themselves into fires long before Native Americans roamed the land, and the fires will continue long after the California coastline shakes itself into the ocean. Nature does its thing, and when we put ourselves in its midst, we are part of its activity. You can always be alert and evacuate when nature acts up in your neighborhood. The meaning of the event, if any, is determined by your relationship to and interpretation of it. As you walk this world, there is a strong possibility you will have the opportunity to experience one of the planet's natural expressions. Don't take it personally; rather, understand the profound lessons you glean from it.

How have you interpreted a disaster in your life?

JOURNAL:

Problem or Project

If you have ever done target practice, you know that you learn as much from missing the center as you do by hitting it. When you miss, you learn how you need to better adjust your aim. Life is about evolving. You discover a great many aspects about yourself when you don't get your way. Defeat or delay is an integral part of the evolutionary process. When you choose to learn from a problem and turn it around, your whole energy field around it changes.

Change your emotion from disappointment to His-appointment. God never fails. The important thing is how you choose to relate to the information life gives you. Before you negatively react to what's going on, lift up your vision. With your head bowed, you can only perceive a dirty, limited world. With your glance lifted, a shift happens—not that things change, but you change, and the shift of your consciousness opens up a new world of possibilities.

What adjustment do you need to make to find the center?

JOURNAL:

A Fly Can Ruin the View

Many of life's hassles are really nothing more than minor nuisances that could be easily dealt with if they were the only things you had to address. The challenge comes when these nuisances start adding up. You can deal with one gnat with a simple swat, but when several are pestering you at the same time, your attention is diverted from the view in front of you. You can have a spectacular view laid out before you, but one pesky bug can capture all your attention.

You have an incredible life with unimaginable possibilities awaiting your selection! Are you able to see this or are you being consumed by minor irritations that have piled up? It may be overwhelming to think of all the areas of your life you have to clean up. If this is the case, put them in proper perspective and then deal with them one at a time, until you have made your way through them. Get started today, and don't let a gnat steal your experience of the Kingdom that lies before you.

Make a list of those irritations in your life that have been adding up and what you can do about them.

JOURNAL:

Watching the Game

You can be free of a wild mind—that consciousness that keeps you reviewing and reliving what has happened and what can happen if things don't go your way. A wild mind can become a daily and nightly energetic stranglehold. Yet, you can be liberated from self-conscious concerns of acceptance and others' perceptions through inward observations. Non-emotional awareness allows you to consciously see your choices from a third-person perspective. Who is making the choice?

Awareness is one of the keys to understanding your consciousness. Being mindful means being able to observe without getting pulled into the experience. When talking about the mind, we often equate it to thinking, problem solving, and the flow of ideas. Too often, left out from these definitions are feelings, sentiments, and instincts. You have the ability to move your attention from an incident with all its linear thought and abstract emotions, to being the container that holds all the aspects of mind. You can watch the action take place on the playing field of life as an observer. You can know that the field of consciousness is not affected by the happenings in your arena. When you remove your attachment to the occurrences and encounters, you view from a distance and make clearer choices.

Where in your life would it be good for you to back up and take a broader view of an emotionally-charged event?

JOURNAL:

Meeting Challenges Easily

As the Spring runoff grows into rivers, it meets millions of rocks along its way. Yet, it has no complaint. Nature unfolds naturally. Patience brings clarity to the strongest path forward. It accepts life and doesn't gripe or feel it needs to force its progress. It may back up sometimes, but only to strengthen its ability to effortlessly move forward.

Sometimes you have to wait for your energy to rise enough to flow over or around obstacles without struggle. Don't waste your time getting worked up and upset, dramatizing your story in great detail. Go inside and allow your energy to gather and lift you above your challenges, leaving behind the rocks in your way as you use the currents of life to easily carry you downstream.

JOURNAL:

Free to Be Abundant

October 1-7
The Joy of Living Abundantly

October 8-15
Joyous Acceptance of Your Good

October 16-23
Joy of Right Living

October 24-31
Joyous Giving

There is So Much to See

Looking out from a mountain ledge at the incredible expanse of scenery, you may see a river that has cut its way through the canyon, rushing through cascading rapids and flowing into a placid lake. Looking another direction, you could see snow-capped peaks reaching from the densely wooded forest toward the heavens. Here and there, you see white-tailed deer enjoying an evening snack in the meadow, while birds sing as the sun settles down behind the mountain, leaving the sky streaked with fuchsia trails, golden rays, and illumined clouds.

You cannot take in the entire vista by looking in only one direction. You cannot see the whole scene in one glance, nor can you experience it all in a minute of earthly time. The experience builds, grows, and expands as the view unfolds. It is just like coming to know the Spiritual Realm. It's all there before you, right now. As you focus on a specific aspect, you come to know that part of the Infinite Terrain. You see the beauty and potential of what is revealed by your focus. Tomorrow, you can go back and study another view, and the next day. another. It will be new each time.

How does the Spiritual Terrain that has been unfolding before your awareness look to you?

JOURNAL:

God as Your Senior Partner

A well-run business includes senior partners who have experience, longevity, and the desire to grow the business for the good of their clients, employees, and themselves. These are the people to whom the company turns in a pinch, in a crisis, or in a time of growth and expansion, trusting that the senior partners have the knowledge, skills, and vision to move things along.

If you think of your life as a well-run business, who can you rely on in a pinch or crisis? Who in your life has the experience, longevity, skills, knowledge, vision, and desire to help you grow? In whom can you place your faith and trust, knowing that they will help you weather challenge or forge prosperously ahead into the future?

With God as your senior partner, you have the wisdom of the ages, the knowledge of the Infinite Presence, the skills and experience of the Universal Principle and Law, and the vision and desire to grow and expand Life itself.

JOURNAL:

No Place Where God is Not

Spiritual life is no different than everyday life. Spirituality reflects how you show up in the everyday activities of your life. The more confidence you have in the Spiritual Kingdom, the greater ease you have in this earthly realm. Things over which you seem to have little control may be happening, but what really counts is what's going on inside of you.

When you take full responsibility for what is going on within, the thoughts that contributed to placing you where you are will change, shifting your interaction with the experience of your world. There is no place where God is not! By putting your focus on Spirit, rather than that which appears uncontrollable, you attract the wisdom to guide the Universe into greater expression. You don't make this Law of Correspondence work; you simply swing your awareness into a different alignment that opens alternative channels for Spirit to move into form.

What's keeping you from bringing Spirit into every aspect of all you do?

JOURNAL:

God as You

You are worth a lot more than your bank account or portfolio. Your wealth includes spirituality, family, friends, health, creativity, and future earning potential. Sometimes in life one can get swept up—or down—in conversing small. When you feel the undercurrent to perpetuate less than God awareness—stop! It is an opportunity for you to step up with a new possibility. There is no reason in the universe for you to be less than you were created to be. There is no reason in the Spiritual Kingdom for God to be less than God expressing Itself.

God is here to show forth Itself as you. It individualizes Its expression appearing as you. You don't express God; God expresses Its own Infinite nature in an abundance of forms that include you. The revelation of your True Identity allows the Word to become flesh, the Infinite and Invisible to become tangible in the way necessary for your life.

Where in your life can you show forth more of your God nature?

JOURNAL:

Beyond Bliss

Meditation quiets your mind and stills the motion of your senses so that you become aware of the Presence of God. Your awareness becomes the place of Divine activity. You are the channel through which Spirit operates. Your thinking mind gives up its stronghold and actually becomes free to receive the Divine impression. You become the individualization of God made manifest.

When you are no longer lost in thought, but free in Spirit, the layers of judgment, doubt, ambition, and self-image fade into the nothingness from whence they came. You'll recognize how common it was for you to have rejected the present in order to maintain the subjective tendencies of the lower self. When your identity drops away, you enter the deepest peace beyond bliss that you can know.

JOURNAL:

Celestial Sounds of Joy

There's more to life than how well you can do a job or how much you get paid for doing it. Life is far more fun when lived in joy. People can get so busy creating their world that they often forget to stop and see the beauty of the world in which they live. All you know has passed through your perceptions. A joyous walk through life is a definite sign that God is present. The way in which you perceive precedes your activity. To get to the place of joy, lose your fears about your work environment and stop thinking about the pay.

The more authentic joy you are free to experience, the more you have. The old, driving, material forces will give way to the greater expression of Spirit. What comes forth from the inner melodies will be celestial sounds you've never heard before. You will have a whole new approach to work, and sharing your gifts will bring joyous satisfaction.

JOURNAL:

"I"

In higher dimensions of being, earthly powers prove to be irrelevant. In a higher dimension, you come to know creation is not by might or power, but by the relaxation of a personal sense into a revelation of the One and Only. You find you no longer need to overcome this world. You are not a separate unit walking around this plane of expression. Spirit is not any less or any more in the visible or the invisible.

By releasing the personal sense of "I," you do not lose the abundant flow of the Universe, but rather place yourself in It. It's no longer the "I" who has to earn a living. Psalms 91:1 says, "Live in the secret place of the Most High." It is here where you have no concern about tomorrow. When Spirit speaks, there is a peace that no one can take from you. "You'll know the peace 'I' give you, the health 'I' give you, the love 'I' give you, the abundance 'I' give you. My grace is your sufficiency."

It is yours to accept or reject. How will you do that?

JOURNAL:

Claiming Abundance

What conversations are you having about money and finances? Remember that what you focus your attention on, grows. When you spend your time worried about your bills or income, you transmit this mental picture to the Universal Principle, which uses it to create the life around you.

Claim your abundance! Claim that the abundance of the Universe is actually the truth of your life. Claim enough money, enough joy, enough freedom, enough of whatever you think you are lacking. You don't need to see it or experience it in order to claim it as the Spiritual Truth. By making the claim, you create a new picture for the Universal Principle to use to manifest in your life.

Journal about the specific abundance you claim for your life right now. Describe it, fall in love with it, and develop it in your imagination until you can taste it.

JOURNAL:

What is Abundance?

Abundance means different things to different people. To some, it's having money in the bank; for others, it's a lot of friends. Some think abundance means a big house in which to entertain family and friends; others find abundance in travel and exotic vacations.

Abundance is whatever allows you to express the fullness of who you are and the life you choose. Abundance is the joy of experiencing a full and rich life, whatever that means to you.

You get to decide what abundance means to you; not what you think it should be, or what your family thinks it should be, but what it is for you. Explore what abundance means to you.

JOURNAL:

Prosperous Living

Everyone is entitled to a prosperous life. Living prosperously means having all your needs met and the freedom to grow into your own fullness. In many parts of the world, people are blessed to live in great prosperity. They have adequate water, shelter, food, clothing, education, and the ability to make a meaningful contribution to their community. In many parts of the world, though, this is not the case.

Take time to really examine how prosperous your life already is. How are your basic needs being met? How do you experience the freedom to grow? Examine the areas of your life where you are not living prosperously. What is keeping you from living prosperously?

JOURNAL:

Talking about Money

"Cold, hard cash." "Filthy lucre." "All you think about is money!" "The love of money is the root of all evil." It is astonishing how many negative things people have to say about money. Yet, everyone wants more of it! Alas, money is necessary in this culture, because it is the basic medium of exchange that we all use.

From a spiritual perspective, money is neither good nor bad. Money is simply the Energy of God, expressing in a form that we can carry around in our wallets. Money is God in Action. It is the energy of God in a visible form.

How do you think and talk about money? Write down some of the things you say. How do they make you feel?

JOURNAL:

Financial Freedom

Most people think they want more money, when what they actually want is to be free to do the things that are important to them—to be free to live the kind of lives they choose. Though this may take money, it may also just take making different choices and deciding what is actually important.

What would you be doing right now if you were truly free from money worries? What would your life look like? What is really important to you today? Five years from now? Ten years?

Now, ask yourself which important things can you start doing today? Do any require money? Do they need as much money as you think? If they do, what are you willing to do to acquire the money you need? What are you willing to start working toward? What choices are you required to make?

JOURNAL:

Placing the Order

When you order something from the menu in a restaurant, you absolutely believe this is what you are going to get. If what is delivered doesn't correspond to your order, you send it back, expecting it to come out correct the next time. It is not your job to figure out how the kitchen is going to do it. You just place the order.

There is a law in the universe that responds to your level of conviction and the order you've placed upon it. This principle says "yes" to the sum total of your belief. Does your inner acceptance contain doubt or worthiness issues or concerns about how it's going to happen? Jesus said that it's done to you as you believe. If you truly understood and believed in the responsiveness of life, you'd make sure your belief systems didn't go unchecked.

What lingering subjective beliefs do you have that could be messing up your order?

JOURNAL:

Deserving Your Good

You are a Child of Light, an expression of Life, an heir to the Divine. This means that you are an heir to the Kingdom of God. This is the abundant life that the master teacher Jesus talked about. You deserve a full, rich, wholesome, happy, sane, and prosperous life.

It does not matter about your background, history or story. It does not matter if you have been abused, sheltered, ridiculed, or loved. It doesn't even matter if you are old or young, fat or skinny, educated, smart, personable, or sexy. All that matters is that you open your heart and your mind to being the best you can be. That is enough.

JOURNAL:

Learning to Receive

When was the last time you let someone take you out for coffee, pay for your lunch, or simply compliment you on what you were wearing or doing? Did you decline? Brush it off? Make it no big deal?

Receiving is a complement to giving and is an important element in the Prosperity Law of Circulation. Joyous receiving allows you to feel your own abundance, as well as allowing another person to practice giving. When you freely receive, you open yourself to more of the good that you desire.

What do you have the most difficulty receiving? How could you accept your good more graciously?

JOURNAL:

Hungry Ghost

The allure of more, new, and better can never be satisfied by the things of this world. Buddhists speak of Hungry Ghost, a big, fat spirit with a voracious appetite and a pinhole for a mouth. Hungry Ghost can never consume enough to satisfy its desires; it always wants more.

Instead of consuming when you want more, you should take a look within to find out why you are not satisfied. When you do what you love and your days are satisfyingly full, you have no void to fill. Your daily creative expression fills you up. If your work is for the money and not the soul, you'll naturally look elsewhere to receive what's missing. Cars, art, houses, and flings will not fill the empty feeling. Only soul-satisfaction will keep you from hungering for the things of this world.

Do you have a void somewhere?

JOURNAL:

Loving Your Bills

Every time you pay a bill, you are thanking someone for trusting you. You are billed for services you have already received, goods you have already enjoyed, and food you have already eaten. Someone trusted you enough to give you what you wanted, believing you were deserving of it.

When you pay your bills with complaints or an attitude, you convey the idea that you are not worthy of the good you receive and not trustworthy enough to pay for it.

Love your bills! Love each company that trusts you. This reminds you to be grateful for the good that you have already received.

Think about paying your bills with a more loving and grateful attitude. Practice doing just that!

JOURNAL:

Landing on Water

When flying, you feel an incredible sense of freedom when you lift off and leave the ground behind. Only one thought might temper this feeling: knowing you'll need a landing strip when it's over. But the more you hang out around water, the more you realize that its surface makes an ideal runway. And the planet contains lots of water! You only need to drop the preconceived notion that you would sink if you landed on water.

Sometimes you need to eliminate a limiting notion in order to acquire a greater realization of what is possible in life. When you finish flying above the turbulence of this world, can you touch down wherever you'd like or do you only have a few environments that work for you? Wouldn't it be freeing to glide wherever your interests call you?

Where in your life are you limiting yourself because you don't know how to get in or out of it?

JOURNAL:

Working to Live?

Sometimes, you work because it is your passion and joy. Other times you work to make money to follow your bliss. This may include volunteer work, artistic expression, or even babysitting children you love on the weekends.

The challenge comes when you simply work to support a life in which you go to work! This can result in coming home every day and watching television, spending the weekends doing chores and watching television, then getting up on Monday morning to go to work so you can pay the television bills. This is not living; it is surviving.

Are you thriving in your life or just surviving? You were not meant to work to pay bills, but to create a life. What life would you like to start creating?

JOURNAL:

True Security

No job pays you enough to sacrifice your dreams. Your only true security comes from experiencing the flow of life. Stock markets crash, savings evaporate, retirement funds disappear, and housing equity becomes non-existent. What seems secure and solid can vanish. When you say "yes" to what is in your heart and live from that, your concerns about saving for the future become irrelevant. When you live a passion-filled life with the Infinite Source flowing through you, true security is yours. Your dreams aren't in the way of your output; they are your way.

When you do that which you were intended to do, you are not looking for a way out. You are the outlet, the activity of God. The whole of God is fully present everywhere, seeking to abundantly flow into expression. Access to this Divine Substance, this untold richness, is through your heart. Don't sell out by doing something you don't enjoy today because you think it will make you secure tomorrow. True security and peace come when the inexhaustible Source moves through you, sweeping away anything unlike It. When you live It, there is nothing in this world that will deny It.

When have you done something for money rather than for your dream? What did it feel like when you followed your heart's desire?

JOURNAL:

October 21

Making a Living or a Life

Work is one of the ways in which you express yourself and give your unique talents to the world. It's also one of the important avenues for directing prosperity into your life. It is intended to be a wonderful and joyous exchange. Is your work joyous?

Work and money are two ways to create the life you want to live. You spend more time at work than you do nearly anywhere else in your life. Is it a pleasurable part of your life or do you simply endure it? Money gives you freedom to do what you want so you can live the life you want. Is money providing you freedom or are you imprisoned by your money?

If you were to focus on making a life and not simply making a living, what would you change or do differently? What would you expand or do more of? What would you keep just the way it is?

JOURNAL:

Working for More than Pay

Too many people work for a paycheck. Let your work be more than a place to earn a living. Allow it to be an opportunity to make a life. This approach keeps you in tune with your life energy, allowing your creative expression to be satisfied. It calls you to bring forth your best. If you lack the desire to bring forth, then you are choosing to cruise because you think you can get away with it.

The point is not about doing what you are paid to do; it's about your growth. It is about the way in which you live with a giving, serving consciousness and get compensated for it. If you cannot work with passion, then quit and find out what makes you happy. No job has a future in it; the future is in the person who does the work. You might look elsewhere for another job, but you'll never escape your self. Your consciousness brings the change, making life wonderful until something else calls you to it. Form follows consciousness, and so do jobs.

JOURNAL:

Hang with God

When do you listen to your fears instead of follow your vision? When do you reject your heart instead of your limitation? If you continue to say "no" to the Spirit of God in you, the heaviness of the world will close in around you. What are you hanging out with, and what are your conversations about?

You will not realize your dreams as long as you believe in your weaknesses. You will always have to deal with what is in your world, but that shouldn't keep you from your ambitions. Claim your freedom, and know that it's not attached to any exterior conditions. Hang out with God, not your fears. Live your life from your vision, not as if it is something in the distance. What can you do now to support your life?

What would you say and do today if your dream was actually happening and you were an active part of what's in your heart?

JOURNAL:

You Are Significant

As you contemplate the ancient trees, the immense oceans, the vast blue skies, the distant, burning stars, you can easily slip into the philosophy that you are insignificant in the scheme of it all. Yet, as you listen to a dear friend pour his heart out, help someone move through her troubles, or say something that changes another person's perspective, you come to realize that you are *very* significant.

You have a choice: to think you don't matter or to believe that you do. Ask your child, partner, or friend if you have made a difference in his or her life. Realize that whomever you affect sends an energetic ripple into the world. You touch more people than you'll ever know. You are significant!

How did you feel when someone told you that you made a difference in his or her life?

JOURNAL:

Giving Freely

Two seas in Jordan are fed by the same river. One is lush, green, and home to many animals and plants—the Sea of Galilee. The other is filled with so many minerals and salts that nothing lives in it or on its banks—the Dead Sea. The only difference between the two is that the Sea of Galilee has an outflow, the Dead Sea does not.

Giving means not hoarding. Giving freely creates outflow. Giving freely reminds you that you have already received so much and there is always more to come. Giving is both an affirmation and an act of gratitude.

Write about your giving practices. Are you giving freely and joyously?

JOURNAL:

Bringers of the Kingdom

Your spiritual awareness is to be used, not flaunted. It is right to walk through this world freely and unencumbered by the temptation to maintain a self-image. When your depth of character is expressed in natural circumstances, you create the world on your own terms, not in response to others' expectations and judgments. You come to know the unexpected joys of life.

When you live with a deep knowingness, you have everything. There is no need to flash it to win respect. You live in a dimension of fulfillment while you embrace your true identity as a child of God. The Adam dream—the human experience—is the sense of separation you feel when you feel you have to go into the world and prove yourself in order to win friends. This is the prodigal existence. Knowing your true identity, you allow your true relationship as an expression of Spirit to be natural and not attention-calling. You no longer seek anything from anyone; you become the bringer of the Kingdom, which will flow forth through you naturally.

How have you done this before?

JOURNAL:

Living in Giving

The teachings of prosperity don't amount to much unless they point you toward a giving consciousness. The purpose of life is not about acquiring, but expanding and sharing your gifts. When giving from this position, you are in the Divine flow. When you see how you contribute to every situation, you call forth the gifts of the Universe.

Too often, people are only concerned with what's in it for them. With this kind of consciousness, there is no way to find satisfaction in the "gimme, gimme" approach to life. With a giving consciousness, you look for ways to share yourself and become a channel for Good. When you give, you find so much more to express from. Life is about being in the joyous flow of expressing God.

When you have constriction, something has to give, and it might as well be you. There is a great blessing and sense of fulfillment from this choice. There is so much Good in you. Let it be your joy and honor to give it away. If your career creates opportunities for you to share your passion, your paycheck will simply be an added gift. The more Good you send forth, the more Spirit flows through you. It knows what you need, what to heal, and how to up-level every aspect of your world. Giving is the key to opening the channel for greater Good to move through you.

JOURNAL:

A Kind Word

Has someone ever given you a kind word—something like, "You're the best!"—that touched your soul when you weren't expecting it? This uplifting soul-shot doesn't come with a hangover or any negative side-effects. This feel-good feeling is a natural high.

Why not pass it on? Since you know how good a kind word feels, can you return one today? Wouldn't you like to make someone feel good about who they are? You may be having a nice thought about someone, but unless you say something, you won't bring the other person any blessings. All you have to do is recognize a good quality in someone and tell them about it. You will be the bringer of blessings through your kind word. An extra bonus is the good feeling sent back your way.

Who would be uplifted to hear a kind word from you? Let them hear it!

JOURNAL:

Paying Yourself

An old formula for tithing dictates ten percent to God, ten percent to you, and the rest to live on. Saving is an important aspect of creating abundance. Saving means paying yourself. This creates greater prosperity in your life, which creates greater freedom and joy.

Saving builds up a reserve. For example, when a beaver builds a dam, the river beneath continues to flow, yet the dam slows it down just enough to create a lovely pond. This pond provides food for the beaver, security for the its offspring, and a lovely place for animals and people to be refreshed.

Imagine that the money you save creates a lovely, refreshing oasis in the midst of your life. How would your life feel with this sanctuary? What do you need to do to get started? If you are already paying yourself, take a moment to sit and be refreshed by your oasis.

JOURNAL:

Tithing with Joy

Tithing is the spiritual practice of consistently giving away ten percent of your income, usually to avenues for your spiritual food. Tithing is a spiritual discipline. The active discipline of tithing on a regular basis gets you into the habit of giving.

Tithing is also a spiritual practice of gratitude. You tithe in recognition of and gratitude for all the good you have received. You tithe to your spiritual community, because you acknowledge that the Source of all your Good is God. Tithing is not an obligation. Nor is it a way to get more. Tithing with joy is the simple act of giving as freely as Spirit gives to you.

How comfortable are you with tithing? If you are not yet tithing, start giving two to five percent and work up from there.

JOURNAL:

The Joy of Enough

Think about the feeling you have after a satisfying meal, one in which you didn't overeat, but savored and enjoyed every bite. At the end of it, you might have said, "I've had enough. I am completely satisfied!"

The joy of enough knows when you are satisfied. It knows that you don't need everything right now, all at once. It means that you are satisfied in the moment with what you have. Noticing when you are satisfied and when you have had enough is a wonderful way to accept abundance and prosperity in your life. And, of course, what you notice and pay attention to, grows!

JOURNAL:

November

Free to Praise God

November 1-8
The Joy of Being You

November 9-16
The Joy of the Harvest

November 17-23
The Joy of Release

November 24-30
Joyous Gratitude

Giving your Gift

You have a precious and unique gift to give Life. It may be your ready laugh, your intelligent mind, your way with children, or your wisdom and insight. It probably isn't just one thing, but whole hosts of ways in which you show up that are uniquely you.

You can give your gift in several ways: through your work or career, through your family, or through your community. Your gift is a big part of why you are here, not what you do for a living—although these two may be combined.

Always know that your gift is necessary right now, otherwise you wouldn't be here to give it.

What gifts are you here to give to the world?

JOURNAL:

Cultural Mecca

Go to any great city and you will find museums filled with fascinating displays, libraries bursting with knowledge, and theaters expressing the culture of the day. As you pass these cultural Meccas, you can feel their call to enter. Yet, every day thousands of people walk by who never even take the time to go in and discover the richness waiting to be experienced.

The richness within you is greater than anything in the outer world. The God display in your inner galleries are just waiting for your discovery. You will be awed by the aesthetic expressions of your being, the wisdom of the ages, and lifetimes of experiences you already possess. You have to slow down, to care enough to make and take the time to visit the mind-boggling, soul-expanding offerings waiting within. To have the transcendent experience of consciousness that awaits your visit, you have to go inside!

What's keeping you from going within?

JOURNAL:

November 3
Your Life is a Gift

God, the Divine Infinite Reality, is within you, expressing as you. You are one of the unique forms in which Spirit shows up in creation. Your life is the gift this Life gives to you.

How are you treating this gift you have been given? Are you loving it? Accepting it? Enjoying it? Or are you criticizing, belittling, devaluing, or abusing it?

Accept and enjoy the breadth of life that is yours. You are free to express it anyway you want. You are invited into the joy of who you are and what you came here to do and be.

JOURNAL:

Loving Your Life

Life is sweet and precious. Your life is the very incarnation of Spirit being and expressing as you. Take a look at your life. Look at the sweet and precious experiences, the beautiful and loving human beings, and the joy and wonder that surround you. Even if you can only find one positive thing, focus on that and bless it with love.

If you do not love things in your life, ask yourself why not. What would need to be different for you to love your life? Are you willing to make those changes? There is no reason for you to be stuck in a life you do not love. Learn how to love those things that are loveable and change those things that are not.

You deserve to love your life and have a life you love.

JOURNAL:

Gifts of God

It is God's good pleasure to give you the Kingdom, but it is up to you to receive it. You are in a land of milk and honey, yet people are starving to death. In a world where so many believe in God, too many seem unwilling to allow Spirit to take them to the next level. What are you waiting for? It has all been given. Where in your life are you not open to the gifts of God?

The task is as simple as gratefully accepting the gift. You can make it more difficult for yourself by claiming that it is "too good to be true." Divine Intelligence knows your need long before you are aware of it, and It has already provided all that is necessary. When you choose to abide in the conscious realization that "all the Father has is mine," you start adjusting to prove that it is true. Your awareness attracts the Good because the gifts of God have already been given, but maybe not specifically to you. The gifts of God are there for all those who have the Spirit dwelling in them.

JOURNAL:

Land of Milk and Honey

This is an infinite, beautiful, awesome life that you live. Sometimes, you may feel like Moses, standing at the edge of the Promised Land, looking in and wondering if you'll actually be able to enter. What kept Moses out of the Promised Land was his inability to believe that all that good was actually his for the taking. He did not believe that God could actually make that happen, so his unbelief kept him out.

Yet, though Moses could not enter, you do not have to stay stuck at the edge. Look around you and see all the places where good is already showing up in your life. Then, realize that if you have already received that much good, how much more the Infinite Reality will provide for you. Nothing is impossible to God, and nothing is withheld from you; all you have to do is believe.

JOURNAL:

Good Luck or Bad Luck

When people talk about a lucky break, they set themselves up to be victims of worldly whims. If you live with the belief of good luck, remember that there is another side of the coin—bad luck. You cannot have one without the other. You have been given unlimited possibilities to call forth that which you desire. Don't give them away to luck.

If you choose to give up your creative power to chance, it is your choice, not that of the Universe. Don't allow the world to shape you into its law of averages. Travel the world knowing that all things work together for your good, even apparent mishaps. Challenges lead you to something better. Some may call it bad luck or good luck, but just make sure you call it *consciousness*.

Where in your life did others see luck when you saw cause and effect?

JOURNAL:

One in a Million

You have a remarkable, precious, amazing, complex, and wonderfully constructed body that has a unique set of thoughts, feelings, and experiences, all of which are contained within the unique way Life is showing up in the world—as *you*. While others may have similar features, backgrounds, or think similar thoughts, no one has put it all together precisely in the way you have. No one ever will.

You are one-in-a-million-billion-trillion! You are one in infinity. Begin to see yourself as special and precious. You are necessary to the Universe for it to be complete, not in an egotistical way, but in a sense that shows you that you belong, that you are important, and that you matter--just like every other unique one-in-a-million being.

What would it be like if you treated yourself that way? What if you treated others that way? Imagine a world full of people who treated everyone that way?

JOURNAL:

The Joy of Manifesting

You are free to create the life you choose. You are free to manifest anything you desire. You may not be able to have everything you want, and certainly not all at once, but you can definitely have anything you are willing to create with your mental and spiritual coin.

The joy of being free in your own life is that you really do get to choose! Some choices, though, have long term consequences. When you choose to have children, that choice may limit other choices until your children are grown. When you choose to pursue a career or live in a certain neighborhood, it means you are not choosing all the other careers or neighborhoods. However, you are always free to re-choose later.

What joy, knowing you have this freedom! In what areas of your life are you enjoying your freedom to manifest? In what areas do you feel stuck?

JOURNAL:

Different Shades of Green

Traveling through the immense Northern Rockies of Idaho, Montana, and Canada, you notice differences in terrain. Variously, you see lakes, rivers, waterfalls, creeks, valleys, meadows, and one hundred hues of green. It would be easy to compare one aspect of the Rockies' beauty to another, choosing which one is better. It is much more freeing, though, to appreciate the distinctive differences as unique and beautiful in and of themselves, without comparison and contrast.

Yes, you have preferences in life—that's what makes life diverse. But you don't need to make other people wrong if their preferences aren't the same as yours. Are you able to hold your point of view without having to make another person wrong? Is it possible for God to appear in your life differently than you expect? Too often, situations and people get characterized in unbecoming ways when they present the opposite point of view from your own.

Where in your life are you proclaiming something as "not good" because it doesn't match your preferences?

JOURNAL:

The Fruits of Your Labor

Your life is the out-picturing of the thoughts, attitudes, beliefs, and actions of your past. Your life bears the fruit of the seeds you have planted. This is both bad news and good news. The bad news is you are harvesting the life you planted. The good news is that if you don't like it, you can plant a new crop for a new harvest.

What fruits are you enjoying? What new seeds do you want to plant?

JOURNAL:

The "Onlys"

Do you find yourself using the word *only* in many of your sentences? "I only have …" "I only earn…" "I can only do…" It is wise to look at where you put the "onlys" in your life, because this one little word has the power to turn off the life flow. It instantly moves your thoughts to what you don't have rather than what you do. It puts you in an attitude of not-enough. Whatever you have in your life, don't let it be attached to *only*. Allow what you have to be identified with the manifestation of Spirit in your life. Know that this is how God shows up. Spirit is a constant flow of Good that effortlessly fills all space. You are the determining factor of the Infinite's manifestations in your world. The objective isn't to get more, rather to take charge of an awareness that leaves the "onlys" behind and uncaps the Infinite flow.

Where are you using the "onlys" in your life?

JOURNAL:

Expecting Demonstrations

Every time you affirm or pray for something, you ought to expect a demonstration. Your spiritual practices are not just things you do to make yourself feel better or to get through rough patches. They are intended to create a better life in alignment with the spiritual truth of who you are. You should expect things to change and improve.

You believe in the power of the Universal Principle, and you know that you participate in the creative process by co-creating your life with Spirit. This means that you can, and ought to, expect your prayers to be answered. Don't settle for anything less.

Expect a demonstration. Pray for it, affirm it, and be grateful for it until it becomes your reality.

JOURNAL:

Upliftment and Eruption

Observing mountains, you see the creative uplifting of two powerful forces colliding. When enough resistance builds up under the earth's surface, it is eruption time. Likewise, when you have disturbances and aggravations in your life, you create a new range of peak experiences for you to explore.

Will you allow your resistance to lift you to a higher vista of possibilities? From a new elevation, you might discover that you really do know what's best for you. What if you find the answer you've been searching for? It's only waiting for an eruption to blow it up through the false perspectives of how you think things should be. Maybe your frustration is the catalyst to blow the lid off, so you can rise to a new level with a solid, mountainous foundation beneath you.

Where in your life would you like to have the top blown off, so you can see what's really inside?

JOURNAL:

Enjoying Your Harvest

The creative process begins with the seed of an idea sown into the soil of the Universe. The resulting plant is an automatic manifestation of the seed. This process reminds us to pay attention to the seeds we plant and to carefully weed our garden.

It is just as important, though, to enjoy the harvest after the planting. Take time to stop and realize how far you've come, how much you've learned, and how fully you've grown and matured. Yes, you may still have rough edges to work out, but you have also begun to reap the benefits of your spiritual and personal work.

Enjoy a fuller life, more meaningful work, and more satisfying relationships. Enjoy the peace you unearth and the path you follow. Enjoy your greater well-being and your deeper relationship to God.

JOURNAL:

What's Coming from You

There will come a time on your journey when you no longer attempt to gain anything for yourself, but rather to reveal the Divine for those who do not see it. Once you have been given the opportunity to see beyond the veil, your responsibility and desire becomes to share that with the world.

This type of sight doesn't come through your personal mind, for the mind is not the knower of revelation. It is a deeper consciousness that rises to the surface of your awareness. The teaching of this is not through words, but deeds. You cannot preach it to the world; you must demonstrate it and let it resonate through your world for others to know that you have been there.

By your fruits will you be known. What "fruit" is coming from you?

JOURNAL:

Joy or Pain—You Choose

Joy and freedom can be as real and natural as sacrifice or struggle. Which do you choose to experience? Though there is pain and death in the world, you can choose to focus on beauty and love. As you stroll through life, you can fill your awareness with the abundant offerings of Good that are ever present. Whether you live in happiness or sadness, it is your choice.

You can feed yourself hearty helpings of drama, living in the seriousness of it all, or you can immerse yourself in the joyous gifts of God. It is all available. You do not need to deny what you don't want; just choose what you *do* want. Life will correspond. That's what it does!

Where in your life have you chosen to see the Good while others pointed to the downside? Were you correct?

JOURNAL:

Joy-Filled and Flowing

Joy is in your hands, not God's. You've been given a key that unlocks the amazing, feel-good flow of Spirit. You already have everything you need to live a joy-filled life, but you are the one who must choose to use your talents. You've been given the strengths to acquire whatever makes you happy. If something makes you sick, why would you keep partaking of it? Follow that which honors your talents.

When you are joy-filled, you are more fun to be around. You tend to be a blessing in the world. You attract Good into your life. When joy-filled, you have more energy to share. When joyous energy and attitudes flow through you, they produce health. Who knows, this might actually be the missing "Fountain of Youth!"

What can you do to get more joy flowing though you?

JOURNAL:

Repeating Patterns

When painting your house, it's easier to just paint over whatever is there, rather than properly prepping it. The problem with this is that you will have the same thing you started with, just in a different color. Before you paint, you need to clean—scrape off old paint, sand, spackle, and wipe down. This can be more time consuming than the actual painting and not the most fun part of the project, but it is necessary.

Life can be easier when you bounce from one situation to the next. Repetitious patterns, though, are like slopping new paint over old paint. It makes little sense to repeat the same problem in a different job or relationship. You might as well have stayed with the old. Floating through life with different people dishing out the same kind of unacceptable behavior toward you is no different than slopping on new paint without properly preparing. You get the same bumps and cracks as before. When it's time for a change in your life, take the time to get rid of the old, built-up history. Scrape away what is no longer of value and fill the gaps. Then, you are not only ready for a new shine, but also a new experience.

Is there somewhere in your life you need to take more time preparing for a new experience rather than just jumping in?

JOURNAL:

Making Space

Nature abhors a vacuum. Just look at how life pushes in everywhere. When you create space by releasing something that you don't need, you make a vacuum for Spirit to fill. Let it! Don't rush to fill the space yourself. If you've released old clothes or let go of old art hanging on your walls, leave the space open for a time. Let it be. You may find you don't need to fill the space.

Rushing to fill the void is the cause of many addictions: over-spending, hoarding, co-dependence. Become comfortable with the open, empty spaces in your life. You will create breathing room for your soul and make room for Spirit to be more creative.

Take some time to make space in your life, your closets, your home, and your mind. Practice being comfortable in the void.

JOURNAL:

Decelerating

Stepping away from what's not working in your life may be powerful, but may come with a lost sense of self and context for being. Embrace the process rather than the battle. It's alright to decelerate for a while when you don't know what to do. It is not a failure to be in the midst of self-discovery. You don't have to know right away or beat yourself up for not knowing. To be in the realm of unknown opportunities can be exciting. In Genesis, God told Abraham, "Get out of your country, from your family and father's house to a land I will show you." God didn't say, "I'm going to give you a map and tell you where the land is." Rather, God said Abraham would know once he got on with his journey.

The Presence which spoke to Abraham is the same intuitive voice looking to be heard by you. It can be liberating to journey without having the absolute knowledge of how it's going to turn out. It's then that you come to discover the magical kingdom waiting for you. To journey inward without a destination heightens your attentiveness and reveals deeper insights. Trust the walk and know you will know when you get there. As you step away from the old aspects of yourself, releasing pieces of clutter from your life which no longer serve you, the you that has long been forgotten will be discovered.

What aspects of your life do you still have around, even though you are finished with them?

JOURNAL:

Letting Go of Stuff

The Universe cannot give you anything new if there is no room for it. If you want a relationship, you have to let go of people who mindlessly take up your time. If you want to have new clothes, you have to let go of those that are too small, too old, or no longer your style.

Hanging on to stuff creates a closed system—nothing goes out, so nothing can come in. Or, if it does come in, it has to be crammed, creating not abundance, but rather the discomfort of clutter, crowding, and over-stuffing.

What can you let go of in your home, your office, your closets or drawers? Keep things with lasting value or meaning, but begin releasing the things you are simply hoarding. As you release these things, practice also releasing old ideas, hurts, resentments, and stories right along with them.

JOURNAL:

Stop and Smell the Pumpkins

Hurry, hurry, hurry! It seems like that's all you do these days, especially in preparation for the holidays. But even the time for getting ready is an opportunity for enjoying life and being present. Being present means you stop planning and worrying about tomorrow, and you stop regretting or reliving the past. You plant yourself firmly in the here and now, looking for what is good in it and enjoying all the good you can.

If you are feeling nostalgic, bring your favorite things from the past into today. If you are worried about the future, do what you can right now, and then let it go until you can do more later.

The only time you actually have is right now. Be here in it. Otherwise, time will fly by so quickly that you will miss it. One of the best mantras you can use is: Be present with what is, right now.

JOURNAL:

Attitude of Gratitude

Developing an attitude of gratitude is one of the most powerful spiritual practices you can learn. An attitude of gratitude includes: constantly being on the lookout for opportunities to be grateful; finding things to be grateful for in the midst of problems or challenging times; and speaking of your gratitude frequently to as many people as possible. This means that you are constantly on the lookout for good, and you name that good when you see it.

The attitude of gratitude helps you not take people and things for granted. It keeps you open and receptive— even a bit humble—which opens the channel for more good to come to you.

Your attitude of gratitude joyfully celebrates all you experience in your life.

JOURNAL:

Counting Your Blessings

Counting your blessings reminds you to be grateful for all you have. Count everything, from the fact that you breathe and have a roof over your head, to all the people and situations in your life that bless you.

You multiply your blessings by counting them, because whatever you pay attention to grows!

List all the blessings in your life that you can think of right now. Then list some more.

JOURNAL:

86,400 seconds

One of those magical times of day is the moment before dinner, when you sit down with your partner or gather with the family around the dinner table, ready to dine together, and you take a unified pause to give thanks and say grace. Of course, you should also take time throughout the day to remember the blessings in your world. There are 86,400 seconds in a day. How many of those seconds have you used today to say, "Thank You"?

Gratitude is an abundant attitude because it comes from a place of already possessing Good. Too often, prayers come from a place of lack. Thus, the prevailing consciousness is, "Something is lacking, and I want to get it." Our vision is a lot clearer when we look from appreciation, rather than need. Remember to give thanks in all things. Not just for objects, but also all situations in your life. There is always space to find something to be grateful for.

Close this journal for a moment and contemplate the many things you have to be thankful for in your life. Then, feel the richness that this awareness brings you.

JOURNAL:

Saying "Thank You"

Most people were raised to be polite, always saying "please" and "thank you." However, not everyone remembers to do this, especially in the business of ordinary life.

Saying "thank you" acknowledges that you see someone for who they are and what they are doing. It means that you notice them and that what they do matters. Isn't that what you want to feel? That's why it is so important to say it to others.

Say "thank you" at home to your spouse, your children, and your parents. Say "thank you" at work to your boss, your co-workers, and your employees. Say "thank you" to the store clerk, the telephone operator, and the person who mows your lawn. Say "thank you" to your friends, the people you volunteer with, your teachers, and your clergy person. You simply can't say "thank you" enough!

Make a list of people to whom you want to say "thank you." Then write or call them.

JOURNAL:

The Joy of Celebrating

There is no greater joy than celebrating life's good fortune. It is equally as wonderful to celebrate someone else's joy. Sometimes, it is equally as hard. We may be embarrassed about tooting our own horn or envious of someone else. We may have trouble accepting compliments and good wishes, or we may have challenges extending well wishes to another, especially if we harbor judgment or criticism.

The spiritual goal is to take unadulterated glee in our good fortune, as well as everyone else's. Remember the glee you felt as a small child when opening your presents or getting chosen for something? You were simply ecstatic! Remember how great you felt when your best friend got just what he or she wanted? That same glee is the joy we can feel for ourselves and for others.

What good fortune can you celebrate with the glee of a child?

JOURNAL:

Seeing the Gifts in Life

Everything that happens in your life is an opportunity for growth and has a gift in it. Your life—who you are, what you've learned, how far you've come—is a product of all the experiences you've had.

Look back over your life, at the decisions and choices you have made. What good do you possess because of them? Look back at decisions and choices others made for you. What good has come out of those?

Everything can be a gift if you expect it to be. When you claim a gift from every experience, the Universal Law of Life must shape it into a gift for you. What gifts are you claiming?

JOURNAL:

Doing Your Thing

When you truly know Spirit is always with you, you don't have to be told in advance what It will do for you tomorrow or the next day. With this kind of knowingness, you can begin every project with a deep trust that it is already a success. But you must begin! You are the conduit through which life moves. Your expression is needed now more than ever.

Forget about what people say regarding your audacity to do your own thing. Your thing is what the world needs now. As much as it may sting to hear peoples' negative statements about your actions, it is far more painful to live your life wondering, "If only I had done..."

What is looking to be expressed through you?

JOURNAL:

December

Free to Celebrate the Light

December 1-7
Joyous Awakening

December 8-13
Joy of Family

December 14-19
Joy of the Light

December 20-26
Joyous Celebration

December 27-31
Joyous New Beginnings

Embracing the Holidays

The holiday season is a wonderful time to joyously celebrate your life, your family and friends, and all the good you've experienced this year. Even if you experienced hardship and loss, you have also seen good. This is the time to focus on that good!

The holidays are only as commercial or overwhelming as you let them be. You can decide to use this time as an opportunity for spiritual practice. You can practice having the joy of God for no reason except to have it. Know that this is the truth of who you are. Practice joyful giving in whatever way you can, however big or small your gifts may be. Practice giving without comparison, without the need to impress, and without any sense of smallness. Practice compassion, unconditional love, and forgiveness. Practice the prosperity of celebrating someone else's good, especially if it is more than yours. Rather than being envious or feeling small, joyously celebrate the good of others. This creates a bigger mental picture in your own life. There are many different spiritual practices from which you can choose.

As you apply these spiritual practices to this season, you anchor them into your life so that they become spiritual practices all year round. Which practice do you choose?

JOURNAL:

Simplicity

Strolling through a house tucked away in the mountains, I noticed the same one-word sign in every room: Simplicity. How have you complicated your life with activities, responsibilities, and financial obligations? Maybe at the time of origination these experiences seemed like no big deal, merely one more addition to your already full world. But how does it feel now? Are you still loving it or is it too much?

One complication we create is taking an intellectual approach toward understanding God. Thought is inherently dualistic. The mind likes to analyze, rationalize, and compare. It is fine to be educated and it has great value, but direct experience is beyond the describable.

Try a simple approach to experience the ineffable and go beyond words. See what your life wants to let go of.

JOURNAL:

Check-in

What good does it do to sail across the ocean when you can't even cross the abyss that keeps you from knowing yourself? It takes time and courage to keep checking in with yourself to see what condition you are in today. It is unrealistic to think your dreams, perspectives, insights, and values of today are the same as they were last year, or even as they were yesterday.

The choices and conversations that satisfy your soul may not be pleasing to others. These expressions can only come from being in integrity with your true self. The challenges and questions arise when you have lost touch with the multi-dimensional aspects of your being, by falling into the routine of the role you've been playing in life.

What shifts do you notice when you take time to check-in with yourself?

JOURNAL:

Grist for the Spiritual Mill

Everything that challenges you, every person who annoys you, every situation that troubles you is grist for your spiritual mill. It can all become grist for your mill when you ask useful questions of or apply spiritual practices to them.

For instance, challenges give you the opportunity to ask, "What assumptions am I making in this situation? What if I see this person as a child of God right now?" They offer the opportunity to go within and be still, practicing compassion or telling the truth.

Every thing, every moment, every interaction is an opportunity for spiritual practice. What is going on with you that is grist for your spiritual mill?

JOURNAL:

The Fall Line

When skiing, one of the keys to effortless turning is to keep your skis in the "fall line." This means keeping them pointed downhill and using the power of momentum to make the turns. When you are enjoying this rhythm, you are "in the zone." As soon as your head gets in the way and you attempt to control gravity by turning your skis uphill, personal effort and strength are required. This creates a lot more work and produces more awkward movement as you attempt to turn from such a slowed-down or stopped position.

When you attempt to get things going, putting together deals or wanting to make contacts, and your creative effort just doesn't seem to be getting you anywhere, that's what it's like trying to make turns without momentum. You have to get back into the fall line. When you are in the flow of life, decisions become clear and life moves swiftly, bringing the right circumstances, people, and funding effortlessly to you. This is what it is like to go with the Power of the natural, gravitational flow of Life.

Where have you allowed your fears to pull you out of the flow?

JOURNAL:

Enlightenment is Not Everything

Enlightenment is a good thing, but it's not everything. After you reach it, then what? People who don't have their finances in order think about money a lot, just as spiritually-deprived people constantly seek fulfillment. Once the financial situations are handled and you are free to function from purpose in the world of form, you still need to have a purpose beyond the want of money. Similarly, when the spiritual connection is clean and one is free to operate in the world, what else must you do besides sitting cross-legged with your eyes rolled back, being blissed-out all day?

What matters is how you move through this world and express your soul's purpose and intention. Your spiritual realization is not the end of your journey, but merely how you walk through this time and space. What you entertain in consciousness becomes evident all around you. An enlightened perspective makes the trip a lot lighter, but it is not the reason for your travels here.

JOURNAL:

Wearing it Down

Can you imagine the sun being upset with you because you stayed inside and didn't go out to enjoy its glorious rays? Then, to show you how upset it was, the sun decided to withhold and not give you light and warmth the next day? Ridiculous concept! It's just as silly to think that God withholds any of Its Good. Yet people "go to God" to ask for something they feel has been withheld. It's like a child working on their parents for a toy and eventually wearing them down to get what they want. Some people approach prayer much the same way; they use their childhood strategy of persistence and making the right promises, so that God will give in and give them what they want.

There is no outside God listening to our pleas. There is no reaching out to anything for anything. So stop waiting for the cosmic postal service to deliver something. It's already been given, and the only way to access it is to live in the fullness of the eternal moment where it already is. Stop looking and reaching for what is already yours. You do not have to earn your Good—just claim what is already yours.

Where are you still attempting to wear down the Universe to get what you want?

JOURNAL:

Loving Your Family

If you are fortunate enough to have a loving, sane, happy relationship with your family, then celebrate it. Bask in the love you share and the closeness you have.

However, the holidays may bring you right up against the feelings, issues, and challenges you have with your family, or certain members of it. This is a powerful time to practice your spiritual maturity.

You might begin with compassion. What flaws do you see in others that you have in yourself, such as lying or bragging or arrogance? This allows you to have deep compassion for someone who is acting purely out of their human limitations and may simply not know any better.

You might practice seeing each person as a child of God, a spiritual being, no matter how they behave. This allows you to love the truth of who they are, without having to love their behavior.

You might practice looking into the mirror. Ask yourself what part you play in all of this? Are you reverting to old patterns? Are you projecting onto another that which you actually dislike in yourself?

Choose one practice for the season, then simply allow yourself to love your family.

JOURNAL:

Creating a Chosen Family

You have a blood family and a chosen family. Your chosen family is made up of those friends with whom you resonate in a deep and intimate way. You may even feel closer to these loved ones than you do to your blood family.

You are free to create a chosen family, especially if you are not closely connected with your blood family. This is not something to feel dismayed about. You can love your family for who they are while being wrapped in the loving embrace of those you choose to be your family.

Spend time celebrating with your chosen loved ones. Honor the connection you have with them. Let them fulfill your need for belonging. Feel the joy of this unconditional love and support.

JOURNAL:

Dealing with Holiday Blues

The holidays can be a challenging time if you don't feel the same joy and cheer you think you should feel. The first thing is to acknowledge that this is how you feel. The second is to create some space in which you can reflect upon the reason for your feelings.

If you are experiencing grief over the loss of a loved one, either through death, divorce, distance, or estrangement, it is so important to acknowledge this grief. Perhaps you have never felt like you've had the happy holidays depicted on greeting cards. It is important to acknowledge this reality. Perhaps you simply feel overwhelmed in your life and can't imagine doing one more thing. It's important to realize that this is what's going on with you.

Journal about your feelings. Acknowledge how you feel and where those feelings come from.

JOURNAL:

Choosing this Side

The thought of checking out of this world may have crossed your mind at some time or another. Occasionally, the lure of being free from the struggles of this existence can seem more inviting than facing them. What about the other side that seems enticing? Freedom from pain? Freedom from responsibility? A sense of peace? The thought of seeing your departed loved ones? The release from earthly responsibilities can, indeed, seem like a breath of fresh air.

Yet this peaceful state is accessible to you right here, right now. The fact that those feelings of freedom have come into your field of awareness means they already exist within you. It is possible to attain a level of peace today. The omnipresence of God means you won't get more God on the other side than you have right here. Our consciousness is an evolving state of awareness. It's about the continuity of the individual soul forever expanding. You attract what's in your heart, wherever you are. The states of being your heart yearns for are already within you. Honor those feelings and they become yours. No need to check out of this place to get them. Whatever prompted those thoughts, too, shall pass.

What can you do now to know this kind of peace and unconditional love?

JOURNAL:

Remembering Loved Ones

Take time this day to remember and honor the loved ones in your life that are gone. Write down their names. Write something about how you feel or what you miss about them.

Thank them for being in your life.

JOURNAL:

Religion or Spirituality

Religion is taught and organized. Spirituality is directly experienced. Spirituality is your connectedness with the Life Force that moves through all things. It's the feel-good feeling you get as you walk through the woods or along the beach, when life seems to be effortlessly flowing through you, and all the pieces seem to come together perfectly.

Even before religion, our ancestors knew this feeling, even though they may have had different names for their inner guidance or higher state of connectedness. Don't be fooled by a pantheon of gods or different paths of religion. Behind all paths is the ultimate experience, the direct union with the Life Force. There is a common thread of truth which has woven itself from the beginning of time through today. The One and only God is trans-denominational. It knows no bounds and is always available to be experienced—yesterday, today, and forevermore.

What religious rules get in the way of your direct experience of God? When did you have a spiritual experience that transcended something you had been taught?

JOURNAL:

The Feast of Lights

"May your days and nights/Be a feast of lights./May you have love." These beautiful words, from a hymn celebrating Hanukkah, offer a beautiful wish for you. May your life be a feast, a banquet of joy and hope, beauty and fulfillment. May your life be filled with light—the light of insight, the light of truth, the light of the Presence of God. May your life be filled with love—the love of family, the love of friends, the love of Life, the Love of God.

Explore the feast of light and love that is your life today. Celebrate the light and love in your life. Contemplate how you can celebrate this all year, not just during the holidays.

JOURNAL:

December 15
All Takes Place Within

Sit and contemplate the sky for a while, and notice what lessons it holds for you. Have you ever been caught in a crazy, tropical storm with dark skies, ominous clouds, and flashes of lighting exploding over the water as the heavens erupt with thunder? It's easy to believe that the storm has an effect on the sky. The truth is, the sky just is; it's open, vast, eternal, and unaltered by what is taking place within it. This storm, too, will pass.

Consciousness, in a sense, is like the sky. The storms, emotions, and stories may come and go. The drama may shake and color your perspective of life, but it really has no effect on the God-consciousness. All takes place within Spirit. Consciousness remains open and unchanged, yet this is where the sight and sound activity of life take place. This does not mean a storm is better or worse than a sunrise, or that one experience in your life is more beautiful than another. It all takes place within the Changeless. All your life's expressions are natural phenomena of nature in the timeless, changeless expression of God.

Where in your world do you need to know that your storms are not really changing the nature of things?

JOURNAL:

Free from Fear and Darkness

Bang the drums, light the fire and torches, sing as loud as you can! Bring in the green boughs and the red holly to decorate the house with life! These are the ancient traditions from mid-winter. These traditions are defiant expressions of faith in Light and Life in the midst of the long, cold days of the season. Lighting fires and hanging evergreens remind us that, no matter how dark and bleak it may appear, this is not permanent. Winter is a necessary fallow time for life to rest and regenerate, so that spring can burst forth in all its glory.

Declare freedom from fear and darkness. Depression, sorrow, a sense of being in the darkness are not permanent, nor does it need to be frightening. You may simply be in a wintry, fallow time. What light do you need to bring into your life to remind you that Spring is not too far away? What drums do you need to bang in order to shake away the fear of darkness? What energy can you bring into your life that will anchor and remind you that Life is *always* present, no matter what?

JOURNAL:

The Hands of God

You may have heard someone ask, "Should I have the operation?" or "Should I trust God to heal me?" These are the kinds of questions that reveal doubt. If there is a concern about God's ability to heal a physical condition, it's probably not going to happen without medical intervention. The truth is, God doesn't heal anything! Your wholeness is already established within the Divine field. All you need to do for it to be revealed is bring your awareness into alignment with the truth of who you already are, irrespective of what's going on in your body. It can be that simple.

Let no one tell you whether or not you should use a medical practitioner. Your body is run by your beliefs and faith, and it is totally your call. There is no judgment around your choice. God works through doctors as clearly as It does through consciousness. Spirit is Omnipresent. If you're not ready to go solely with spiritual practices, that's fine. Regarding your body, it is wise to listen to your consciousness and not someone else's idyllic perspective.

Where is the edge of your belief?

JOURNAL:

Celebrating the Light

Celebrate the Light...
   of Insight,
   of Enlightenment,
   of Clarity,
   of Hope,
   of the Presence of God,
   of Illumination, of Truth,
   of Christ Consciousness.

What Light are you celebrating? How is it showing up in your life?

JOURNAL:

Hearing Beyond Words

The more in tune with the Infinite you get, the quieter you become with your spoken words. You reach amazing perceptual heights of understanding. Your learning seems to come from nowhere and you see a clearer truth. But don't attempt to convey these new insights through the spoken language. Words are not the clearest vehicle for communicating Spirit. They can point people in a direction, but there are few who can hear beyond words or who are willing to spend the time it takes to get to the timeless.

Enjoy what you know. Let the Divine Gift express as you in all you do. Be the Truth you know, showing forth your inner nature in all you do. What you do not give, you do not have. When you share through your actions, from your connection from beyond, you will be lifted to a realm of higher activity. Show the way by living life abundantly, healthy, joyously, and filled with love.

Where in your life can you show this truth in a greater way?

JOURNAL:

Where is Your Bethlehem?

The nativity story unfolds in Bethlehem during the birth of the Christ child and symbolizes the birth of Christ Consciousness within you. Each character and place in the story reminds you what is needed to make a place for the birth of the Christ Consciousness within: a pure heart (Mary), a committed spirit (Joseph), a quiet, humble place (the manger). The birth is attended by Spirit-centered Consciousness (angels) and awe-filled Wonder (shepherds). Gifts of Spiritual Insight (myrrh), Power of the Word (frankincense), and Co-creation (gold) are given for this birth. And it all takes place in the spiritual center of your being (Bethlehem).

The Christ Consciousness is the reality of your Oneness with God and the seat of your spiritual essence and power. This Consciousness is available to each and every person. It already resides at the spiritual center of your being. Spend time in your Bethlehem, making sure there is room for your own rebirth.

JOURNAL:

December 21
Within is Not a Place

The only place you have to go to find God is within. Within is not a place, but an awareness. God is consciousness, Infinite Consciousness. This Omnipresence includes your consciousness and is the substance of all things. To the degree that you awaken to the knowingness that there is not Spirit and you, but God *as* you, you leave behind the humanhood of struggle.

You will no longer go to God for things, because your awareness understands the One Power. The fight between form and Spirit dissolves. The wisdom of the Divine emerges, not as an impartation from a teacher, but as an expression of God's Grace.

Where would you like to give up the fight between form and Spirit?

JOURNAL:

Shepherds and Angels

Myths have archetypical images within them to guide you on the path to freedom and joy. The nativity story is filled with this type of imagery.

Angels are messengers of God. They represent intuitive insight and spiritual guidance. Your intuition is the place where Spirit speaks and you listen. This is why the angels appear to shepherds. Shepherds remind us that humble acceptance and willingness to be guided are proper attitudes to take toward intuition. The shepherds didn't question the angels; they simply followed the guidance received from them.

What guidance are you receiving? How are you following it?

JOURNAL:

Bundled in God

Sitting alone on a ski chairlift, bundled in warm ski clothes, heading toward the top of the mountain with snow falling from the heavens creates a magical moment. The majestic, white scenery, the fully flocked trees, and the profound silence while traveling through the sky make time disappear. There is only this magnificent moment, and everything else disappears. Whatever was so important is left behind and holds no significance in this moment. Only joy and fun await your arrival at the top.

Imagine if you took off each day from home, bundled in the warm feeling that you were protected from the swirling elements of life, prepared to actually appreciate God's hand in the storms, equipped to traverse the steep places, thinking it was all fun. You'd use boulders in your path to make fancy turns, and, when launched into the air, you would hoot and howl with excitement, landing with grace and momentum.

Let the exhilaration of your day be considered fun, because it reveals your skill at bringing your spiritual connection to life's terrain. Just as skiers don't improve unless they find their edge and take a few falls, so will you improve as you take a few spills. The key is to get back up and get going again, knowing you have what it takes because you are bundled in God.

In what storms of your life do you need to see God?

JOURNAL:

Spirit's Incarnation As You

Christ Consciousness is the incarnation of Spirit as you. It is the Holy of holies at the core of your being. It is the truth of your nature and the reality of your life. As you spend time preparing your home for the holidays and gifts for your loved ones, you are preparing your consciousness. You do your spiritual practices to clear out your mental closets, open your heart, clarify your thinking, and prepare for the awakening of the Christ Consciousness.

What preparations are left? Take the time to consciously determine what you still need to do to make room for this rebirth.

JOURNAL:

You're the Gift

You are such a gift! There isn't another person like you, nor will there ever be. Your unique expression is a contribution to everyone you meet. You are a child of God, and you blessed this world the day you arrived. The angels sang and the stars shone brighter. You have been endowed with Divine Qualities that bring joy to the world.

Today, unwrap the most precious gift you have—you. Leave nothing in the box. You've been given whatever it takes, so don't forget the accessories you have for all occasions and circumstances. Remember where your gift came from—God. Spirit knows what you will need even before you do. Trust the greater Intelligence that has birthed you into being, and know you are a light to the world. Let it shine!

Where are you holding back you gifts and talents, and what can you do to share them?

JOURNAL:

Peace on Earth

This is a powerful time to honor peace in your life and in the world. Peace on earth begins with peace in your heart and mind. This grows into peace in your family, which translates to peace in your community. Peace in your community leads to greater peace among the nations and all people.

Who do you need to make peace with? Where do you need to find peace in your community or in the world? Are you carrying around resentments, judgments, or anger that prevent you being at peace with others?

When you find you are at peace in your mind and in your life, you become a powerful force for harmony. Intend peace for people everywhere. Imagine that the peace in your own life is the truth of everyone's experience. Hold peace in your consciousness and you will become a healing force in the consciousness of the world.

JOURNAL:

Qualities to Live By

The Seven Principles of Kwanzaa are—

Unity: Success starts with unity—unity of your family, community, nation, and race.

Self-Determination: To be responsible for yourself and create your own destiny.

Collective work and responsibility: To build and maintain your community and to help those within your community.

Collective economics: To build, maintain, and support your own stores, establishments, and businesses.

Purpose: To be responsible to Those Who Came Before (your ancestors) and to Those Who Will Follow (your descendants).

Creativity: To use creativity and imagination to make your communities better than they were in the past.

Faith: To believe in your people, your families, your educators, your leaders, and righteousness.

Explore these qualities and how you live them in your own life.

JOURNAL:

The Power of Prayer

The spiritual discipline of personal prayer opens doors to your soul so that it may commune with the Divine, remembering where you come from and reminding yourself of where you are going. Personal prayer takes many forms—praise, gratitude, blessing, creation, lamentation, and adoration. Prayer can be mute or ecstatic, quiet or formal, whispered or sung.

Pray with an open heart, an open mind, and a willingness to be moved. Pray with an ear to the ground of your being and an eye to the vastness of the sky. Pray with words you make up, words you have read, curse words, gentle words, love words, and words that wring profound feelings from your soul. Pray as if you life depends on it. Everyday. Because it does.

Every breath is a prayer; every heartbeat is a prayer; every word you utter or thought you obsess about is a prayer. Explore the spiritual discipline of personal prayer.

JOURNAL:

Welcoming the New

Are you feeling stuck in your life? Are you like a gerbil, running on an endless wheel of repetition? Have you become so comfortable with the ruts of your life that you've repaved them?

It may be time to practice welcoming newness into you life. Welcoming newness is like inviting a new friend over. You host your new friend with the best you have, and you work on getting to know them.

What if you did this with something new in your life? What would that new thing be? How would you host it? What is the best you could give it? How would you find out all you could about it?

Welcome in the new by making space in your life and room on your calendar. Create willingness in your heart.

JOURNAL:

Awakening to the Future

The future beckons, bright, shiny, and new. The future is home to your hopes and dreams. These hopes and dreams are the lines you cast into the future. Through faith and consistent effort, you use them to pull yourself toward that future.

What hopes are alive in you? What are you dreaming about? What are you willing to do today to move in that direction?

JOURNAL:

December 31
Invite in the New!

As the old year comes to an end and the New Year approaches, now is the perfect time to do a little bit of self-assessment. Reflect on this past year and make the following lists:

Three triumphs you had.

Three things for which you are grateful.

Three things you are ready to leave behind.

Three things you would like to forget or be forgiven for.

Three things you will forgive and not carry into next year.

Three things you are planning to do

Three things you to which you are looking forward

What else do you want to reflect on?

JOURNAL:

Acknowledgements

Blessings and gratitude to:

Edward Viljoen and Chris Michael for the idea and inspiration; Heather and Bruce Pedersen who opened their beautiful retreat center, Talus Rock in Idaho, for mountainous inspiration; Kathianne Lewis for the inspirational setting where we decided to team up; Joanne Millison who proofread every word Christian wrote (and changed a few); Heather McKay for organizing text and Kathy Farrer proofing all our words; Randall Friesen, a wonderfully encouraging and clarifying editor; and our families and friends for their continuous love and support

About the Authors

Christian Sorensen

A gifted and eloquent speaker and author with a unique and engaging style, Christian lights up audiences all over the world with his expansive vision, passion, and heart-felt enthusiasm. Christian has authored four books, numerous articles and pamphlets, and hosted two television shows on practical spirituality, New Thought, and growing one's consciousness. Christian leads spiritual tours and works with orphanages and schools around the world to raise global consciousness. Christian's intention is that his life be his message.

Rev. Christian Sorensen, D.D., is the spiritual leader of the Seaside Center for Spiritual Living, Encinitas, California. His weekly talks can be viewed at www.seasidecenter.org.

Petra Weldes

A highly-regarded, deeply-admired teacher and speaker, Petra engages others with her deep wisdom and wealth of knowledge—as well as humor—awakening others to their unique expression and creative and joyful potential. Petra has authored numerous articles and led countless retreats on Spiritual Living. She has a passion for youth, interfaith service, global transformation, and expanding consciousness. Petra speaks at conferences and leads sacred site journeys around the world. Petra's intention is to grow people and things into their greatest purpose and self-expression.

Rev. Petra Weldes, D.D., serves as spiritual leader of the Center for Spiritual Living, Dallas, Texas. Her messages can be heard at www.csl dallas.org.

For more information on Spiritual Living, Science of Mind, and a practical, positive spirituality that teaches tools for personal transformation and making the world a better place, go to either of the websites listed above. To find a community in your area, go to www.united centersforspiritualliving.org.